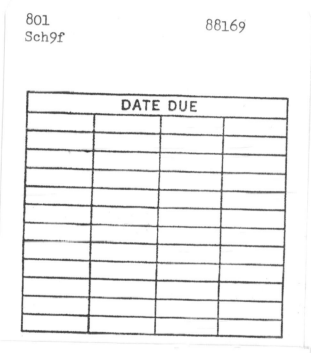

DATE DUE			

The Forms of Feeling

KENNIKAT PRESS

NATIONAL UNIVERSITY PUBLICATIONS

SERIES ON LITERARY CRITICISM

General Editor
EUGENE GOODHEART
Professor of Literature, Massachusetts Institute of Technology

The Forms of Feeling

Toward a Mimetic Theory of Literature

Elias Schwartz

National University Publications
KENNIKAT PRESS
Port Washington, N.Y./London/1972

Library of Congress Catalog Card No.: 74-189561
ISBN: 0-8046-9020-0

Manufactured in the United States of America

Published by
Kennikat Press, Inc.
Port Washington, N.Y./London

For Marjory

FOREWORD

EACH OF THESE essays deals with a particular problem in literary
theory, and each seeks a solution through the study of concrete
cases. I make certain theoretical assumptions throughout, but
some of the assumptions in later essays are established in earlier
ones. I hope that when the reader has reached the end of the
book the outlines of a theory of literature will have begun to
emerge.

The topics I deal with seem to me central ones: they are
nearly related to the problems of the critic in his attempts to
understand particular works and the nature of his own methods.
Throughout I am concerned with theory as it illuminates criticism, with particular works as they illuminate theoretical issues.

From the start I make use of a number of key ideas first
enunciated in Aristotle's *Poetics*. Let me say that I am not trying
to elucidate Aristotle. I am, alas, not qualified to do so. Nor do
I believe that Aristotle is an infallible guide to truth. I do believe
that certain Aristotelian concepts are especially useful to the
literary theorist. I would therefore wish the reader to regard my
persistent appeals to the *Poetics,* not as proofs from authority,
but as a way of developing a consistent approach to the problems under discussion.

Except for the concluding chapter, each of these essays was
originally published, usually in shorter form, in periodicals.
Chapters I, II, III, and VIII appeared in the following issues
of *College English:* XXIX (February 1968); XXXI (November 1970); XVIII (December 1956); XXI (January 1960).
Chapters V and VI appeared in *Criticism* VI (Summer 1964)
and XIII (Spring 1971). Chapter VII was published in *Shakespeare Quarterly* XVI (Winter 1965). Chapter IV originally
formed part of a controversy with W. K. Wimsatt and Monroe C.
Beardsley. It was entitled "Rhythm and 'Exercises in Abstraction'" and appeared in *PMLA* LXXVII (December 1962). I
am grateful to the editors of these journals for permission to use
this material.

CONTENTS

The Forms of Feeling

CHAPTER ONE

MIMESIS AND THE THEORY OF SIGNS

I

WE BEGIN WITH an attempt to understand the meaning of *mimesis,* or "imitation," as it is usually rendered in English. Though this concept is, in both Plato's and Aristotle's theory of art, a master concept, its meaning has received relatively little sustained study. The reason for this is not clear: It may be that the idea is simply too slippery to handle; it may be that its meaning is usually assumed to be self-evident.

In his fine book on the *Poetics,* Gerald F. Else points out that Aristotle is not, as most commentators have believed, addressing himself to the nature of poetry in its usual modern senses: as referring either to an abstract essence or to the aggregate of all poems.[1] Aristotle is concerned, rather, with the art of making poems. The distinction is not trivial; it has ramifications for the interpretation of the *Poetics* as a whole. In this and in other ways, Else's book is fresh and invigorating, especially for those who continue to take Aristotle seriously. On the vexing question of *mimesis,* however, Else is disappointing. He does not, as we might expect, put his scholarship and acuity to the task of grappling with this key concept and the problems raised by it.[2] And once again the meaning of *mimesis* is neglected. Yet if anything could restore a mimetic theory of literature to the respectability it deserves, it would be a thoroughgoing study of this concept.

Mimesis is not defined or explained by Aristotle, and our difficulty in understanding it is compounded by his rather slippery use of the term. In the first chapter of the *Poetics,* he uses it to differentiate the poetic arts (including music) from other productive arts (house-building, harness-making, etc.). What dis-

1

tinguishes the former is their *mimetic* nature: "The writing of epic
and tragedy . . . and most of the art of flute and lyre—all these
are . . . forms of imitation." *Mimesis* here, according to Else, has
some of the verbal force of *poetike*.[3] That is to say: it involves
the idea of making or creating. It seems fairly evident that it also
(as in most of its other uses) includes the idea of a *relation,*
either between the activity and some object, or between the
product of the activity and some object. An imitation, in brief,
is an imitation *of something*. It is this relationship which needs
elucidation, and it is just here that Else fails us.

We want to know several things. What exactly *is* the activity
which *mimesis* refers to? How is it accomplished with *words*?
And *what,* exactly, does the poet imitate? Else does not attempt
to answer the first two questions. As to the third, he seems to
assume that the object of imitation is simply some part of external reality.[4] But this assumption, though common enough, is
neither warranted by the text of the *Poetics* nor plausible in
terms of our experience with literary works. It is true that when
he refers to the object of imitation, Aristotle often speaks of
"men in action" or human "action"; but it is not at all certain
that he means outward physical deeds. Furthermore, when he
speaks of rhythm as a means of imitation, he says that its object
is characters, emotion, and action. If we consider carefully the
idea of a play imitating an actual person doing something, it
soon appears to be an absurdity. Does *Othello* imitate an actual
man doing and suffering? But Othello (the man) does not exist;
he is created by the play. Surely a play cannot imitate itself.

It is not possible to separate in thought the process from the
object of imitation, not possible to answer questions about the
process without assuming some view of the object. Yet, the limitations of human discourse being what they are, we must speak
about process and object separately. We begin, then, with the
process.

How, exactly, does the poet imitate? This is not the same as
asking: What is the nature of poetic language? The latter question assumes that the distinguishing feature of poetry lies in some
peculiarity of its language and necessitates an answer in those

terms. This is the way most New Critics and descriptive linguists with an interest in criticism approach the matter. For most of the New Critics, poetry is a kind of *discourse;* for the descriptive linguists, it is a species of *language.* In either case, the essential question is begged and the real issue concealed. If we can agree that poetry is an art, then we ought to begin by placing it in the class of imitation, and then distinguish it from other members of that class. We should not begin by assuming that poetry is a kind of language or discourse, and then distinguish it from other kinds of language or discourse—which is what New Critics and descriptive linguists regularly do.

The procedure being urged here is, of course, the procedure of Aristotle. He starts by placing poetry in the class of imitative arts and then distinguishes it from other such arts in terms of its *means.* For Aristotle, its means are language, rhythm, and melody. We may be surprised at Aristotle's inclusion of rhythm and melody here; but he clearly thinks of the "poetic arts" as including instrumental music and he also has in mind the musical interludes of drama.[5] If we adhere to our own classifications and exclude instrumental music and song from "poetry," we are left with language and rhythm as the means of poetry, for both prose and verse *have* rhythm, and rhythm alone is a means of imitation, as in dance.

Rhythmic imitation is a special problem which we may put aside for the moment. For the present let us say that poetry is a form of imitation which is distinguished from other imitative arts in using language as its means. If we accept this view, it seems (again) to follow that *we cannot find the essential nature of poetry in some intrinsic peculiarity of its language.* We must look, rather, for a peculiarity in its *use* or *function* in poetry. The question is: What makes poetic language *imitative?*

At no particular period in the history of the English language has there been an intrinsic difference between the words and the syntax of poetry and those of ordinary speech. Certain poets may use a special diction or syntax, but few critics today would maintain that there is anything intrinsically poetic in Milton's Latinate diction and syntax. By the same token, there is nothing intrinsically poetic in language which is ambiguous or emotive or image-provoking—though any such feature may indeed be present in the language of a poem or of many poems.

II

Before turning to the question of poetic *mimesis,* let us consider the term as it applies to all the fine arts. One aspect of the idea of *mimesis*—a very obvious one—is that the process and its product are *artificial.* Unlike the creations of nature, the creations of art do not "contain" their own formal and efficient causes. These causes inhere either in the artist or in his art. Art, says Aristotle, "is a principle of movement in something other than the thing moved, nature is a principle in the thing itself . . ."[6] Again: ". . . from art proceed the things of which the form is in the soul of the artist."[7] It is in creating after the *manner* of nature that art imitates nature.[8]

From a slightly different viewpoint, *mimesis* is artificial in that it involves the imposition of a form on matter which is not natural to that form. The statue of Socrates is made of marble, not flesh and blood; the landscape painting is made of pigment and canvas, not wood and water and grass. Obviously, *mimesis* involves formal similarity between its product and what it represents; yet, in its "material" artificiality, it also involves *dissimilarity.* And our perception of this dissimilarity cues an aesthetic response—a response to a work of art rather than a response to an actuality. We know that the statue is not a man, that the landscape is only a painting.

There is also a *formal* dissimilarity between the art-work and what it represents. The statue of a man is not quite in the form of a real man; the painted tree is significantly, if slightly, different in form from a real tree. There are important implications of this which we need not take up at present; for now we need only note that our perception of this difference exposes assumptions we have been making all along. We have been assuming that the work of art imitates some perceptible, extra-artistic reality and that "to imitate" is literally "to copy."

It is on the basis of just these mistaken assumptions that Eliseo

Vivas rejects the theory of imitation: It denies, he says, "the creativity of the poet."[9] Vivas' objection is valid, however, only if one assumes that art copies external reality. Then the artist is indeed superfluous, for the tape recorder or camera can copy nature more exactly than poet or painter. The simple-copy theory also implies that the value of a work resides in its fidelity to external reality, not in some inherent excellence—and this is palpably false. The fact that *mimesis* involves dissimilarity as well as similarity also argues against any literal view of imitation.

III

It seems, nevertheless, inescapable that the idea of *mimesis* entails the idea of *transitiveness*—that there is *something* which is imitated. What is not self-evident is that the "something" is a physical thing, something external, sensuously perceptible. Nothing in the *Poetics* indicates unambiguously that the "something" is physical. In Chapter I, Aristotle speaks of those who "imitate and represent various objects through the medium of colour and form, or again by the voice." But "objects" here would seem to be generic: it means "the things which are imitated." Other passages suggest that the "object" is *not* a physical thing, but a spiritual or psychological entity. Aristotle speaks of rhythm and melody as imitating such inner realities: character, feeling, states or activities of the soul. And since these media (rhythm and melody) bear no resemblance to any physical reality, we may surmise that their "object" is an inner or immaterial one.

I shall take the position that the object of imitation, not only of melody and rhythm, but of poetry, in this inner reality: a structure of feeling, in Aristotle's terms, a movement of the soul. Of course, the poet also imitates (creates the illusion of) an external reality (men doing or saying things); but this, I shall argue, is only a stage, an intermediate phase, of the imitative process. The poet imitates plot, character, or human speech as a *means* of imitating the movement of the soul, which is his ultimate object.[10] (Rhythmic imitation, which we shall take up later, bypasses the intermediate stage of imitation.)

This view of the ultimate object of imitation is essentially that

of Susanne Langer, as Vivas notes.[11] It is also the view of Francis
Fergusson. After pointing out that Aristotle conceives of "action'"
as different from "plot," Fergusson explains that "action" (*praxis*)

> does not mean outward deeds or events, but something much
> more like "purpose" or "aim." Dante (who in this respect is a
> sophisticated Aristotelian) uses the phrase *moto spiral,* spiritual
> movement, to indicate *praxis.* In Aristotle's own writings *praxis*
> is usually rational, a movement of the will in the light of the mind.
> But Dante's *moto spiral* refers to all modes of the spirit's life,
> all of its directions, or focuses or motives, including those of
> childhood, dream, drunkenness, or passion, which are hardly
> rationalized at all. . . .
>   Aristotle . . . and Dante . . . seem to imagine the psyche much
> as an amoeba looks under the microscope: moving toward what
> attracts it, continually changing direction or aim, and taking its
> shape and color from the object to which it is attached at the
> moment. This movement is "action": and so we see that while
> the psyche is alive it always has action; and that this changing
> action in pursuit of real or imagined objects defines its mode of
> being moment by moment.[12]

The ultimate object of poetic imitation, then, is action in this
sense. It is not an outward, but an inner reality. It is, in Aristotle's
terms, a movement of the soul, in Langer's, a structure of feeling.
It is not mere emotion or sensation; it includes all modes of the
psyche's activity. It is embodied in the poem, and it is called into
actuality in the responding reader or spectator. It is what the
poet imitates, and it constitutes the poet's vision and the meaning
of his poem.

IV

The mimetic process in the poetic arts is more difficult to
understand than it is in the other arts because the poet's medium
is language, and language has a multiplicity of common uses
other than the making of poetry. Our ordinary use of language is
self-expressive or practical: We use it to record or convey ideas
or feelings, to persuade or to plead or to console, or merely to
pass the time of day. It is in terms of such uses that we are habitu-
ated to language. And this habituation tends to interfere with our
understanding of its mimetic use, for in none of the uses men-

tioned do we use language mimetically. Only the poet does that; that, says Aristotle, is what distinguishes him *as* a poet.

How, then, does the poet use words mimetically? One answer must be ruled out. We cannot say that the poet copies the speech of men in actual discourse. Clearly, the poet creates speech which has some *likeness* to actual human speeches; but poetic speech is also *unlike* actual speech. If the poet only aimed to copy actual speech, then he might well abandon his art in favor of the tape recorder, which can copy more accurately. Every actual speech would be a perfect imitation, and the poet need not take thought about shaping language into some form, for eloquence and "natural" utterance are equivalent. (A good deal of "realistic" literature aims for just such "eloquence.")

If we examine some lines of English poetry:

> They flee from me that sometime did me seek
> With naked foot stalking in my chamber. . . .

> Shall I compare thee to a summer's day?
> Thou art more lovely and more temperate. . . .

> For Godsake hold your tongue, and let me love,
>   Or chide my palsy, or my gout. . . .

> When first thou didst entice to thee my heart,
>   I thought the service brave. . . .

> The soul selects her own society,
> Then shuts the door. . . .

> Turning and turning in the widening gyre
> The falcon cannot hear the falconer. . . .

> Lay your sleeping head, my love,
> Human on my faithless arm. . . .

we may note (1) that these utterances "sound like" human speeches—we can imagine, we are induced to imagine these lines being spoken; and (2) that these utterance are *not* like ordinary, casual English speech, that they are in fact *artificial,* fictive speeches.

The Russian Formalist, Victor Shklovsky, has argued that the be-all end-all of art and the distinctive feature of poetic language is the de-automatization of perception. Art exists, he says,

> that one may recover the sensation of life; it exists to make one feel things, to make the stone *stony*. The purpose of art is to impart the sensation of things as they are perceived and not as they are known. The technique of art is to make objects "unfamiliar," to make forms difficult, to increase the difficulty and length of perception because the process of perception is an aesthetic end in itself and must be prolonged. *Art is a way of experiencing the artfulness of an object; the object is not important.*[13] (Shklovsky's italics.)

There appears to be some ambiguity in Shklovsky's theory as to just what the "object" of perception is. And we may find a curious opposition among theorists on this matter: for some the function of artistry is to facilitate the mind's passage *through* the medium; for others (as for Shklovsky) its function is to inhibit or slow down this passage and to focus attention on the medium itself. My own view is that poetic language does "defamiliarize" and so intensify perception, but that this serves a further end in facilitating our perception of what the work "means," of the poet's vision.

In each of the opening lines of the poems I have quoted, the language is such that we are led to infer a "situation," a person speaking, thinking, feeling; and at the same time, we are made aware that this situation, this speaker, this speech, are *not* actual, are fictive. The language in these poems is being used mimetically —to make poems.

V

In order to analyze with more precision the process of poetic *mimesis,* we need to use a more precise terminology than that generally available in literary discourse. Such a terminology is provided by the scholastic theory of signs. Let me sum up the points in this theory which are relevant for us.[14]

The scholastics define the sign as that which makes known to a cognitive power something other than itself. *Signum est id quod repraesentat aliud a se potentiae cognoscenti.* The sign takes the place of the thing to which it refers, and it makes this referent present to the mind. Thus nothing can be a sign of itself; a sign must *refer*—must stand for something else. And it makes this other thing *known*.

There are *natural* signs and *conventional* signs. The natural sign is found in nature, is not created by man. Smoke, for example, is a natural sign of fire. The relation between smoke and fire is intrinsic and necessary; they are connected by a natural and unalterable causal connection. The conventional sign, on the other hand, is made by man. The word "dog" is created by man to refer to the concept and the animal of which it is the sign. The relation between sign and signified is purely arbitrary; any other sound would serve as well, so long as it is agreed upon by the language-group and so long as it does not "interfere" with other such auditory signs. In the case of both the natural and the conventional sign, the sign takes the place of the signified and makes the signified known. And in either case, the sign is *a thing in itself,* something sensible, apart from its function as sign. It becomes a sign as soon as it serves to signify.

This suggests the distinction made in the scholastic theory between *instrumental* and *formal signs*. All signs, except the concept, are instrumental signs. The concept is a formal sign because it has no physical being; it has only intentional being, it exists only insofar as it conveys meaning.

Of particular importance for us are the distinctions the scholastics make between *signs, images,* and *symbols*. An image is something that has formal resemblance to some other thing. It is not necessarily a sign. A son may be an image of his father, but he is not a sign of his father. In order to be a sign, an image must be "artificial"; that is to say, its matter cannot be natural to its form. If an image is also a sign, it is called a *symbol*. Thus the statue of Socrates is a symbol: at once an image and a sign of Socrates. It would seem that any product of mimetic art is a symbol—though what it images and signifies remains a sticky problem. (The statue of Socrates symbolizes a living or dead man; but what of the statue of Apollo or Hamlet?)

The scholastics distinguish, finally, between *direct* and *reverse* signs. We have so far been concerned with signs which *refer to objects*. These are direct signs; they differ from reverse signs, which *make known a subject*. A reverse sign must also be a direct sign: It cannot make known a subject unless it also makes known an object—unless, in other words, it has meaning. Its primary function, however, is to make known a subject—in the case of words, to reveal the thought, feeling, and character of the speaker. All words, all speech, insofar as they imply a speaker, have some reverse signification. It would seem that, in literature, reverse signification is particularly prominent, since in lyric poems and in dramatic speeches, we get the revelation primarily of the inward presence of the fictive speakers of such poems and speeches.

VI

A work of poetic art is made of words: conventional, instrumental signs. These signs are organized into complex patterns of various sorts: into sentences, verse paragraphs, narratives, dramatic speeches—in accordance with grammatical, rhetorical, logical, psychological or dramatic principles. These elements, the verbal structures at this "level" of organization, are further organized into more complex structures: into a poem or a novel or a play.

The words of a play are made into sentences and into dramatic speeches; they thus "become" the speeches of the fictive persons of the play. These speeches have direct signification; they also have reverse signification: they express the feeling, thought, character (the fictive human presence) of those who speak them, of those who, in a sense, are "created" by these speeches. These speeches, further, with all the meanings which they contain and express, are arranged in a certain temporal order (expressing a causal and dramatic order) which constitutes a *plot*. And this complex, multi-leveled structure, which is made of words but which is supra-linguistic in nature, is a play.

This play is an *image:* a complex structure made of words which represents, images, creates, some sort of fictive human action or experience. It is an image because it bears a formal likeness to such experience: And it is also a sign because it is artificial, made of words, and because it has *meaning*. It is therefore a *symbol*. But a symbol of what?

The play is an image of a certain sort of human experience. But the experience is fictive, just as the persons of the play, what they do and say, are fictive. What, then, can the play signify? It seems absurd to say that it signifies itself. Yet it seems clear that the play means *something*. Just as the speeches of the persons of the play signify both directly and indirectly, i.e., just as they refer us to objects in order to express subjects, so the play is a (direct) image and a (reverse) symbol. As image, it refers us to actual life: not to actual persons, but to actual human feelings, attitudes, activities; it does so in order to signify in reverse the *meaning* of this image. The play images (represents, "makes believe") the actual in order to signify the fictive world of the play and its inner meaning.

This inner meaning is the *action* that the play imitates. It is not an external actuality, but neither is it unreal. It is a spiritual reality, a movement of the soul, a pattern of feeling. The play is a symbol of this action, which is in the play *in potentia* and which is actualized in the responding spectator. One point about the medium: When the words of the play "become" dramatic speeches, conventional signs (words) become *natural* signs (feeling, thought, character). In other words, thought, feeling, attitude, etc. are expressed by conventional signs (words); but thought, feeling, gesture and deed are *natural* signs of human character and human action. Speech, of course, is "natural" to man, though it is composed of conventional signs. (It is just this equivocal status of speech which leads to confusion about the nature of poetry.)

It is almost impossible to illustrate adequately the process I have been describing because of the interpenetration of all the "levels" of a play's structure. It may be helpful, however, to attempt an analysis of a particular passage.

The words in Hamlet's soliloquy—"O that this too too sullied flesh would melt"—are conventional, direct signs. "Flesh" refers to the substance that composes the human body. (In its context, however, it is a synecdoche for "body.") As an element of Hamlet's dramatic speech, it is a reverse sign, referring back to the speaker's body. The sentence of which the word is a part is also a sign—a composite one—with direct and reverse signification. It directly signifies the desire for death; as a reverse sign, it signifies Hamlet's particular longing, as qualified by the thought and feeling of the rest of the passage. The whole soliloquy is a *natural* sign of the fictive speaker's character, attitude, and thought. *All* of Hamlet's speeches, as qualified by every other element in the play, create the *image* of Hamlet as a fictive person.

Thus all of the words of the play, patterned into sentences and into speeches of distinctive kinds, create images of fictive persons standing in certain relations to one another and doing or suffering certain acts. These fictive persons and their doings and sufferings, structured into a certain temporal sequence constitute a complex sign-image or symbol; this is the play, *Hamlet,* which imitates a distinctive action, which is the meaning toward which *all* the elements of the play aim.

This analysis makes clear, I think, that particular dramatic speeches, images of character and act, and the symbol which is the play—that these are all dependent for their precise nature on the language (on diction, syntax, imagery, rhythm) which, at the "beginning" of the imitative process, are the *means* of their production. That is to say, the character of Hamlet or the precise effect and meaning of a scene are *functions* of the language which creates them and, indeed, of all the language of the play. And the precise nature of the play's action and its meaning are functions of its language.[15]

VII

The lyric may also be analyzed as a structure of signs. It, too, is "dramatic" insofar as it always implies a speaker and a situation, specific or general. It differs from drama most obviously in its greater compression and in its consequent greater dependence on logical, rhetorical, and prosodic sources of power. The lyric does not aim at the creation of illusional reality, at the development of character and plot. Yet, through the art of language and the art of rhythm, it too imitates human action.

The language of the lyric, like the language of drama, is from one point of view (the linguist's) indistinguishable from the language of ordinary speech. Its words are conventional signs, surrogates for the concepts and objects to which they refer. It is always in terms of a poem's direct signification that we begin to make out its literal meaning, its paraphrasable content. The first line of Donne's *Holy Sonnet I*—"Thou hast made me, and shall thy work decay?"—might be paraphrased: "Will you, my Creator, let me die?" But this, like all paraphrase, misses the full meaning of the line in its context.

Seen in its context, as part of an imitation, the line implies a speaker and a situation. Near despair, terrified by death and the probability of his damnation, the speaker pleads—almost demands—that his Maker give him the grace he needs for salvation. We make these inferences by interpreting the words of the poem as reverse signs, signs which reveal the speaker's character, feelings, thoughts, and spiritual condition. The mind of the reader "moves through" the *direct* signification of the words to their *reverse* signification, and then to a grasp of the poem as a whole, to a grasp of the poem as symbol: finally, to the action which the poem imitates and its meaning.

As we read the poem, we know that we are reading and responding to a fictive utterance, to an imitation, not an actual prayer or a discourse about Divine Grace. How do we know this? Partly because we are aware of certain conventions—meter, the sonnet structure, the carefully wrought syntax—partly because we perceive that the primary signification of the words is reverse rather than direct—they convey a *subject,* rather than being *about* something. One result of this awareness that the poem is an imitation is an intensification of attention: we attend more closely to the words even as direct signs than we might otherwise do. Our perceptions are thus indeed "de-automatized," and we attend and respond more intensely to the fictive experience embodied in the poem than we would to an actual one.

Let me put the whole poem before the reader.

> Thou hast made me, and shall thy work decay?
> Repair me now, for now mine end doth haste;
> I run to death, and death meets me as fast,

And all my pleasures are like yesterday.
I dare not move my dim eyes any way;
Despair behind, and death before doth cast
Such terror, and my feebled flesh doth waste
By sin in it, which it t'wards hell doth weigh.
Only thou art above, and when t'wards thee
By thy leave I can look, I rise again;
But our old subtle foe so tempteth me
That no one hour myself I can sustain.
    Thy grace may wing me to prevent his art,
    And thou like adamant draw mine iron heart.

Once we have grasped the literal meaning of the poem, we may then understand the poem as a dynamic image: the image of a terrified man engaged in fervent prayer. As the fictive prayer unfolds, we discern the spiritual "movement" of the speaker's soul (the action which the poem imitates). He "moves" from the desperation of the opening lines to a recognition of his sinfulness and helplessness without grace (lines 3–7), to an awareness of God's power to help him despite his sinfulness (lines 9–12), to the chastened humility of the half-plea half-hope of the concluding couplet, which implies his ability now (at the end of his prayer) to co-operate with God's grace. The poem is thus a fictive prayer which "actually" works.

We may note, furthermore, a tendency to focus more intensely on the contextual reference in the poem than we would in the drama, partly because we are aware that the poem *is* a poem, partly because of its compression and contextual complexity. The poem begins with the image of the speaker on his death bed, and then evokes the other meanings of death—sin and damnation—meanings dramatically and for a Christian naturally associated with the initial meaning. At one point the meanings coalesce: "my feebled flesh doth waste/ By sin in it, which it t'wards hell doth weigh." And then the brilliant adamant-iron figure at the end gathers into itself the notion of the speaker's inveterate sinfulness, the "weight" of his sins and his sense of being dragged down to damnation, his need for grace to pull him up, the irresistibility of God's grace, unseen but always operative, the speaker's sense of his unworthiness, and the mysterious affinity—the mutual attraction—between the speaker's soul and God.[16]

Narrative fiction would seem, at first glance, more difficult to analyze than the lyric in terms of the theory of signs—especially third person narrative. In such a narrative, persons and events are told *about,* rather than presented direciiy as in drama. Characters, except for passages of dialogue, are not *impersonated* (one of the subordinate meanings of *mimesis*), but described, reported. Yet the novel or the short story is clearly an imitation of human action. What distinguishes these forms is simply that they present action indirectly: The reader infers the inner action, the subjective, from what is objectively given.

We need not here distinguish the varieties of narrative method, the ways of positioning the narrator with respect to his story and his reader. Typically, the words of the novel "create" images of persons, places, events, and these are structured into a complex verbal symbol which imitates a human action. This symbol is similar in most respects to a dramatic symbol; it differs most obviously in lacking the immediacy—the visual and auditory actuality—of drama, and in utilizing an anonymous narrative "voice" or a distinctive persona to tell the story.

How do we know that we are reading a novel and not a work of history? *The Return of the Native* begins: "A Saturday afternoon in November was approaching the time of twilight, and the vast tract of unenclosed wild known as Egdon Heath embrowned itself moment by moment." There follows an elaborate description of the Heath, some commentary on its history, some philosophizing about its nature. No human being appears, nothing happens, until Chapter II. Yet we know that this is fiction. How?

Our first signal is the indefiniteness of the time: "A Saturday afternoon in November. . . ." This is really a matter of convention; the one in question here is a convention about *beginning* a story. (The most conventional and formulary of all beginnings: "Once upon a time. . . .") The fictionality is also indicated by the "progressive" verbs. Something is "going on"—even though no event is referred to. The Heath is presented *as if* it were *there* before us, and both the "as if" and the "presentness" indicate that what we are reading is a work of fiction, and not a work of history or something else. We are aware, furthermore, that we are listening to the voice of an anonymous narrator who is capable of knowing and seeing all. (A literal impossibility, this is perhaps the most basic of all narrative conventions.) Once we are aware of the fictionality of what we are reading, the philosophizing "falls into place": We know that the Heath will be the scene of the story we are about to hear.

Pride and Prejudice begins: "It is a truth universally acknowledged, that a single man in possession of a good fortune, must be in want of a wife." A long sentence, developing this piece of wisdom, follows, and we might well anticipate an essay on the subject. But what we get is this:

> "My dear Mr. Bennet," said his lady to him one day, "have you heard that Netherfield Park is to let at last?"
> Mr. Bennet replied that he had not.

And so on; for the rest of the chapter we get a dialogue focused on the question of a potential husband for one of the Bennet girls, a dialogue which also conveys the characters of Mr. and Mrs. Bennet and gets the plot going. In both the Hardy and Austen passages there is expository prose, a kind of language which we usually associate with pragmatic uses of language, not with literature. Yet in both instances the expository is *subordinate* to its imitative function—so that it becomes a part of the imitative structure. In both passages, fictionality and the imitative status of the language are signalled by the *pretense* of reality and by the convention of an omniscient narrator. However expository a novelist may at first glance seem, his expositions become part of a structure which is essentially imitative. The novelist, like the poet, is thus an imitator of human action by means of language, a creator of verbal symbols.

VIII

Verbal *mimesis* is clearly not a kind of speaking but a kind of making, a making with words. By thus defining poetry as a kind of *mimesis,* we place it (where it belongs) in the class of "fine" arts, and we may then differentiate it from other fine arts in terms of its means: language. Most of the New Critics hold to a *linguistic* theory of poetry. They start from the assumption that poetry is essentially a kind of speech or discourse, differing from other kinds of speech or discourse in its possession of some special "poetic" quality or feature. For Cleanth Brooks and Robert Penn Warren, who represent the standard New Critical view, "Poetry is a form of speech, or discourse, written or spoken.[17] It is differentiated from other kinds of discourse in terms of its subject matter, its organic nature, its "full exploitation of the resources of language.[18] For Brooks, poetry is essentially linguistic: a kind of discourse which differs from other discourse by virtue of its irony or paradoxicality.

Though he admits his dissatisfaction with his own and other New Critics' theories of poetry, John Crowe Ransom, too, defines poetry as a kind of discourse. It differs from scientific discourse, he says, "by bringing into experience both a denser and a more contingent world, and commanding a discourse in more dimensions.[19] For Yvor Winters, poetry is "a statement in words about a human experience.[20] It differs from scientific statement in its capacity for conveying with precision the emotion that ought to attend a rational understanding of the experience with which it deals. R. P. Blackmur alone of the New Critics appears to see poetry as essentially mimetic. Referring to I. A. Richards' linguistic approach to poetry, he remarks that "it can handle only the language and its words and cannot touch . . . the imaginative product of the words which is poetry: which is the object revealed or elucidated by criticism. Criticism must be concerned, first and last with the poem . . . as what it represents is felt.[21]

The attempts of linguists to use their concepts in literary criticism seem to me invalidated by their failure to define poetry adequately. The linguist sees a work of literary art as a subspecies of language, as a kind of verbal discourse. But since a poem is not *essentially* "a linguistic fact," since a poem is *essentially* an artifact or imitation, linguistic concepts are simply irrelevant to it. The metrical structure of verse is an aesthetic, an artificial structure, not a "natural" one. The language of a poem is transformed by its function within that aesthetic structure. It is therefore inappropriate to apply, for instance, the Trager-Smith system of suprasegmental description to English verse—

though this system may indeed be accurate and illuminating in the analysis of English *speech*. So also in the analysis of style: Nothing significant (for the literary critic) can be learned merely by determining the frequency of certain linguistic categories in the prose, say, of Faulkner's *The Hamlet*. What is significant is the relation of his style to the formal structure of the novel, its function in imitating the novel's action.

The linguistic theory of poetry has, in the practice of some critics, produced critical insight and illumination. But the theory itself is invalid. The surest sign of its invalidity are the muddles into which it leads, when those who espouse it come to deal with important problems in criticism and theory. The validity of the mimetic theory, on the other hand, is certified by its capacity to clarify or solve the same problems. That, at any rate, is one of the things I hope to demonstrate in the chapters that follow.

NOTES FOR CHAPTER ONE

1. Gerald F. Else, *Aristotle's Poetics: the Argument* (Cambridge, Mass., 1957), p. 9. I shall use the term "poetry" throughout in its generic sense.
2. Else, pp. 12–13, 96–101.
3. Else, p. 12.
4. This is the meaning assumed by Eliseo Vivas when he attacks the theory of *mimesis*. See his "Animadversions on *Imitation* and *Expression*," JAAC XIX (Summer 1961), pp. 425–32. The meaning proposed by Roman Ingarden in "A Marginal Commentary on Aristotle's Poetics—Part II," *JAAC* XX (Spring 1962), p. 284, is essentially the same.
5. *Poetics* I.1447a. I shall use Butcher's translation throughout.
6. *Metaphysics* XII.3.1070a (trans. A. Platt).
7. *Metaphysics* VII.7.1032.
8. *Physics* II.8.199a. See also *Metaphysics* 1034a: "Things which are formed by nature are in the same case as these products of art. For the seed is productive in the same way as the things that work by art."
9. Vivas, p. 426.
10. Else (p. 237) seems to interpret Aristotle's "parts" as *stages*

in a process—which is what I am trying to suggest here. See also Francis Fergusson, *"Macbeth* as the Imitation of an Action," in *English Institute Essays: 1951,* ed. A. S. Downer (New York, 1952), p. 33: "In a well-written play ... we should perceive that plot, character, and diction, and the rest spring from the same source, or, in other words, realize the same action or motive in the forms appropriate to their various media."

11. Vivas, p. 429.

12. Fergusson, pp.31–33.

13. V. Shklovsky, "Art as Technique," in *Russian Formalist Criticism: Four Essays,* ed. L. T. Lemon and M. J. Reis (Lincoln, 1965), p. 12.

14. For a more detailed exposition of the scholastic theory of signs, see *The Material Logic of John of St. Thomas,* trans. Simon, Glanville, and Hollenhorst (Chicago, 1955), pp. 388–404; and Jacques Maritain, "Sign and Symbol," in *Redeeming the Time* (London, 1943), pp. 191–198.

The scholastic theory seems to me more generally valid than the frankly behavioristic theory of signs developed by Charles W. Morris. For Morris' theory, see his "Aesthetics and the Theory of Signs," *Journal of Unified Science* VIII (1940), pp. 131–50; and *Signs, Language and Behavior* (New York, 1946).

15. If this analysis is valid, that is, if the various levels of poetic structure are inter-related and inter-penetrating in the way I have described, then it would seem that any critical method which focuses exclusively on one level, without taking into account its relation to the others, is defective. Neither the New Critical focus on language nor the Neo-Aristotelian focus on plot is wrong in itself. Each may be a valid method to the extent that it recognizes that the level on which it focuses is related to other levels of the work's structure.

16. It is clear from this analysis that the response of the reader is not, strictly speaking, a "response to words on a page"—which as Reuben Brower points out, is an assumption behind most New Critical analysis. See Brower, "The Heresy of Plot," in *English Institute Essays: 1951,* ed. A. S. Downer (New York, 1952), p. 47.

17. *Understanding Poetry,* rev. ed. (New York, 1956), p. xxxiii.

18. Ibid., pp. xxxvii, xxxviii, xlix, 582–583.

19. *The New Criticism* (Norfolk, Conn., 1941), p. 330.

20. *In Defense of Reason* (Denver, 1947), p. 11.

21. *Form and Value in Modern Poetry* (New York: Anchor Books, 1957), pp. 358–59.

CHAPTER TWO

LINGUISTICS AND LITERATURE

I

FOR SOME FIFTEEN years now linguists have been trying to bring the methods of their science into useful contact with literature. They have not met with much success, chiefly, I think, because they have failed to distinguish clearly between the object of literary criticism and the object of linguistic analysis, between the structure of language and the structure of literature. I take such a distinction to be self-evident, though it is a difficult one to define precisely. One reason for this is that literature is *made* of language. From one point of view, therefore, a work of literature may be regarded as a chain of sentences. That, I believe, is the (proper) viewpoint of linguistics; but as soon as one so regards a literary work, it ceases to *be* a literary work and "becomes" a linguistic text merely. That, in brief, is why linguistic analysis is not, and cannot be, literary criticism.[1]

A 1964 stylistic study by M. A. K. Halliday illustrates the limitations of one kind of "linguistic criticism." All texts, says Halliday, "including those . . . which fall within any definition of 'literature,' are accessible to analysis by the existing methods of linguistics."[2] Of course all texts are "accessible" to such analysis. But will such analysis tell us anything about the *literary* structure of a literary text? By treating poems as pieces of language, Halliday insures the irrelevancy of his results—their irrelevancy, that is, to literary criticism.

Halliday's analysis of "Leda and the Swan" and a passage from *Morte d'Arthur* is chiefly a count of recurring linguistic features in the two texts. He sums up:

"Leda and the Swan" shows a high proportion of verb words in the less verbal structural positions. Moreover, the more lexically powerful . . . the verb item, the less verbal its use. . . . In both these features this poem stands in sharp contrast to the passage of Tennyson. . . . The greater part of "Leda and the Swan" is made up of nominal groups: these nominal groups contain 46 out of the 56 lexical items in the poem. Of the mass of lexical material in the modifiers and qualifiers, almost none is defining; this in spite of a high frequency of those very deictics, especially "the," whose normal function is precisely to identify such material as defining. We do not need linguistics to point out that Yeats' treatment of an event here is very different from Tennyson's. But we do need linguistics between the two texts.[3]

Are the differences here either stylistic or literary differences? These relative frequencies, it seems to me, tell us only that they are what they are. Halliday makes no attempt to relate them to the poetic structure or meaning of the texts in which they appear. And they do not, so far as I can tell, represent the "felt" formal features which a good reader would note in trying to account for the differences between the two texts.

There is no basis for comparing the Yeats poem with the Tennyson passage. They are not of the same genre—except on the assumption that verse constitutes a genre. And there is a telling equivocation in Halliday's use of the word "differences." It seems to refer to literary and linguistic differences at once. One infers that Halliday does not see a distinction between literary and linguistic structure; he does not, in any case, even suggest that there is a level of structure beyond the linguistic one. Halliday's procedure is not unlike explaining the differences between a man and an ape by comparing the number of bones and muscles in each body. The statistics may be accurate, but they will not aid understanding.[4]

The virtues of the linguist as critic have been recently urged by Roger Fowler. Admitting the inadequacy of early attempts at linguistic criticism, Fowler is nonetheless optimistic about the future.[5] He believes that linguistics is now much more sophisticated than it was in the Trager-Smith period; now "the repertoire of statements we can make about the language of literature is much wider."[6] In order to be a good literary critic, the linguist only needs to make the proper adjustments of his methods.[7] "To be critics," he says,

> we must be competent linguists, and then become less of linguists. The development of precise techniques, the theorizing in linguistic terms, though essential, carry us only a short distance. A programme for linguistic criticism cannot be proposed in terms of a theory of language only. After the refinement of methods, and some thought on elementary questions (literature is basically a use of language, a literature is part of a particular language, etc.) all remaining issues are critical problems.[8]

Fowler seems to be espousing here the position I urged a moment ago, but this appearance is deceptive. For one thing, the most crucial question in this context is begged in the casual definition of literature as "a use of language." Elsewhere Fowler concludes that it is not possible to distinguish between literature and non-literature. "This conclusion must be of prime importance to the linguist, for it relieves him of the necessity of making special assumptions about the nature of literary form."[9] But if that is true, there is really no point to calling for *literary* theory, as Fowler does.

Fowler is thus caught in a dilemma of his own making. He sees the inadequacy of a purely linguistic approach to criticism, but he can define no other approach. Halliday's method, he says, will disqualify linguistics "from contributing significantly to literary criticism," because it is unselective.[10] The linguist therefore ought to use "hunches" to focus his analysis of literature.[11] But what is needed is not hunches, but a theory either distinguishing linguistic from literary structure or showing the relation between linguistic and literary categories. Fowler does not seem to have such a theory.

The linguist, Fowler remarks at another point, "must make a *whole* analysis of the literary text, and must then proceed to utilize his analyzed and understood fragments as elements in a synthesis."[12] But Fowler has no way of defining literary wholes, since on his own showing such wholes are indistinguishable from strings of sentences. The linguistic "fragments" he refers to can be synthesized only into sums. Thus at the root of his difficulties lies his view that linguistic structure cannot be distinguished from literary structure.

Fowler is not alone in this dilemma. So far as I can judge, linguists have generally felt compelled to regard literature as strings of sentences in order to bring their methods to bear on it. But this is to reduce literature to language; and a *literary* feature, which is not a linguistic feature, "will escape by this very fact the methods of linguistic investigation: for linguistic methods, the features of the literary language are no more than linguistic features pure and simple."[13]

II

But is literary language different from ordinary language? Literature, as one cannot help seeing, is made of language. And many critics define literature in terms of some special feature or quality of its language. If literature is definable in linguistic terms, if we can discern some intrinsic difference between the language of literature and ordinary language—then linguistics *could,* taking this difference into account, be used for the analysis of literature. Let us attempt to answer this question; but first we need to set down a stipulative definition of literature.

I do not equate literature with the use of a particular style. Nor do I include in this class essays like those of Arnold or Carlyle or Lamb, or histories such as those by Gibbons or Thucydides. I mean "imaginative" or mimetic works that use language as primary medium; novels, short stories, lyric poems, dramas, epics. Thus *Paradise Lost* qualifies, but not *Areopagitica; A Modest Proposal,* but not Pope's *Essay on Man.* I do not wish to defend this definition; I only want it to be clear and unambiguous. I shall be content if, literature being so defined, I am able to discover in its language an intrinsic difference from that in ordinary use.

I think we may dismiss as distinctive of the language of literature what are essentially *semantic* qualities. New Critics, though they are often thought of as formalist critics, tend to fix attention on such features. Paradox, irony, ambiguity—these are all features of meaning, rather than formal, structural features of language. Furthermore, there is sometimes ambiguity in the writing of New Critics as to the locus of these features. Cleanth Brooks in a famous essay asserts at one point that a certain poem gets its power "from the paradoxical situation out of which the poem arises."[14] Yet in the same essay he also says (p. 8) that the paradoxes in a poem "spring from the very nature of the poet's language." This discrepancy is not explained, and it appears to me that Brooks' real concern is with the paradoxicality of the experience or the total meaning of poems. But paradox (or irony, ambiguity, plurisignification) may also be found in non-literary texts or speeches; so that such features cannot be distinctive of literary language.

I think we may also rule out the notion that literature is distinguished by a special diction or syntax, different in some degree from the diction and syntax of standard speech. We may rule this out as a distinctive feature of literary language, even though it is obvious that some literary works do in fact depart from standard diction and syntax. The point is that other literary works do *not* contain such departures. Thus Hemingway's novels and short stories are markedly paratactic and virtually without highly abstract words; Dreiser's novels, on the other hand, are written in a prose virtually indistinguishable from ordinary speech. Yet both Hemingway and Dreiser write novels.

The fact that there are in some literary works obvious departures from standard syntax and diction is explainable in terms of *foregrounding*. According to Prague School theory, foregrounding is the key to literary or poetic language; it is what distinguishes such language from the standard and ordinary uses of language. Yet it is clear that foregrounding occurs frequently in non-literary texts and in ordinary speech, with various kinds of rhetorical effect.

The theory of foregrounding is most persuasively set forth in Jan Mukarovsky's essay "Standard Language and Poetic Language."[15] Mukarovsky does not give a formal definition of literature; he simply focuses on the relation between standard and "poetic" language. His main thesis is that the systematic violation of the norm of the standard language;

is what makes possible the poetic utilization of language; without this possibility there would be no poetry. The more the norm of the standard is stabilized in a given language, the more varied can be its violation, and therefore the more possibilities for poetry in that language.[16]

Now, as I have already pointed out, the "violations" referred to here can occur in texts that are far from poetic in any usual sense. They occur in journalistic prose, in academic lectures, even in casual conversation. Mukarovsky recognizes this, but he maintains that such foregrounding "is always subordinate to communication: its purpose is to attract the reader's (listener's) attention more closely to the subject matter expressed by the foregrounded means of expression."[17] In poetic texts, on the other hand, foregrounding is used "in order to place in the foreground the act of expression, the act of speech itself."[18] This notion, that literature is distinguished by "a set toward the message as such, focus on the message for its own sake," is rather common among linguists.[19] And, for Mukarovsky, this is ultimately what distinguishes poetic from non-poetic language, not the presence or absence of foregrounding merely. But in making this distinction, Mukarovsky appeals, not to an objective linguistic feature, but to a psychological function; and he invokes a distinction between communication and perception which would, I believe, be very difficult to demonstrate. I, at any rate, cannot believe that what distinguishes literature is that it merely intensifies our perception of the act of speech itself. On the contrary, I should say that literature communicates *par excellence*—though just how and what it communicates is not easy to describe.

One function of foregrounding, not mentioned by Mukarovsky is its signalling of fictivity. This is obviously one of the functions of meter, which is, curiously, both a conventional automatization and a linguistic foregrounding. Generic conventions, conventional devices of all sorts, have dual functions: They signal the fictive status of the text even while they provide extra-linguistic norms which increase the resources of poetry. But in every case the language so used is not *in itself* distinctive. It is the same language that may on occasion be used in non-poetic texts. To argue that its *function* is different is truly to beg the question.

We must therefore reject Mukarovsky's theory as a key to distinctive poetic language.

III

I argued in Chapter I that literature ought properly to be classified as a species of *mimesis* rather than as a species of language or discourse.[20] The choice of genus here is not indifferent or a matter of mere personal preference. Definitions may be more or less apt, heuristic, in accord with the "facts." Now if one wants to find out something about a work of literature, one must try to define it in terms of what distinguishes it from all other objects. To classify it as a form of language is to distinguish it from all non-linguistic objects; but it is also to make it *similar* to all other linguistic objects. And then, as we have seen, it is very difficult to distinguish it from those objects. This is, I think, a sign of the wrongness of the initial classification. There is also something inherently wrong, I think, with classifying so complex an object as a work of literature primarily on the basis of its "matter." We would not do this with the other fine arts. We would not, if we were interested in understanding painting or music as such, define painting as a species of pigment or music as a species of sound—though we might indeed do so if we were interested in color phenomena or acoustics. When linguists define literature as a species of language, they make it indeed accessible to their own science; but they also make it inaccessible to literary criticism.

I hold, therefore, to the view that what essentially defines literature, and what aligns it properly with the other fine arts, is Aristotle's old idea of *mimesis*. And what distinguishes it from other mimetic arts is its medium, language. But then, assuming the validity of this classification, we may still ask whether there is anything distinctive about the medium. To put the matter precisely: Is there any objective feature that distinguishes language used mimetically? Is its mimetic function marked somehow in the language of literature?

Robert Frost's "Stopping by Woods" begins:

> Whose woods these are I think I know.
> His house is in the village though;
> He will not see me stopping here
> To watch his woods fill up with snow.

Now what can we say about the poem's language? It is rather simple, colloquial language, language that might be used in ordinary conversation. The first line is "inverted"—and so departs slightly from standard syntax. And the language is set to meter—though if we take each clause out of the metrical context, it will no longer be patently metered. Apart from this, there is nothing here (or in the rest of the poem) which might not be considered quite ordinary *as language*. Yet the poem is mimetic, like other poems, and it is made of language.

The language of Frost's poem is functioning mimetically. That is, we are led by it to infer a speaker, a situation, a speech—all fictive. It is clear from the second and third stanzas that the speaker is aware of the oddness of his stopping there. It is also apparent that the woods are not merely beautiful to him—they *symbolize* something.

> My little horse must think it queer
> To stop without a farmhouse near
> Between the woods and frozen lake
> The darkest evening of the year.
>
> He gives his harness bells a shake
> To ask if there is some mistake.
> The only other sound's the sweep
> Of easy wind and downy flake.

What the woods symbolize is death; and so we know that the speaker yearns toward death (though we do not know why). This interpretation is certified by the last stanza:

> The woods are lovely, dark and deep,
> But I have promises to keep,
> And miles to go before I sleep,
> And miles to go before I sleep.

Here the opposition in the first two lines focuses the feeling and the action of the whole poem: though the speaker longs for death, he decides stoically to resist its appeal until all his "promises" have been kept.

Thus we infer not only a situation and a speaker, but an action and its meaning. None of these inferences depends either on metrical setting or syntactic irregularity. Yet they are *contained* somehow in the poem's words. Since the inferences, the mimetic function, are not dependent on either the diction or syntax, we are led to the conclusion that they depend rather on *the total structure* of the poem. The words of the poem are ordinary words, that is to say, but they attain mimetic status by their place in the poetic, not the linguistic, structure of the poem. We have a curious phenomenon. Words, ordinary words, are used in such a way that they *make* what is essentially an aesthetic, not a linguistic, structure. And this aesthetic structure confers on the words of which it is made a mimetic function, a function *which is not marked in the words themselves.* And it seems that we know that the language of the poem is functioning mimetically, not from any feature inherent in the words, but from our sense of the total poetic structure and our perception of the relation of parts to whole within this structure.

It now appears that the qualities which have been attributed to literary language or which have been said to be distinctive of it—paradox, irony, polysemy, foregrounding, etc.—are not distinctive of literary language—though they may in fact be present in the language of this or that poem. What distinguishes the language of literature is not some inherent feature, but its function in relation to the whole of which it is part. This function is not marked in the language so used; it inheres rather in the relation of that langauge to the total structure of the poem, a structure which is aesthetic, not linguistic. There is no such thing as a distinctive literary language. And if this is true, it means that, though linguists may tell us a great deal about language, they can tell us nothing about literature.

NOTES FOR CHAPTER TWO

1. I am referring in this paragraph to American "structural" linguistics and to British "levels-and-categories" linguistics based on the thought of J. R. Firth. It is these two schools which have produced the attempts at linguistic criticism which I examine in this chapter. Chomskian linguistics (the transformational-generative school) has not, so far as I know, concerned itself with literature or literary criticism. One of the earliest statements by a structuralist is the Harold Whitehall article cited in note 5 below. See also Archibald A. Hill ("An Analysis of 'The Windhover': an Experiment in Structural Method," *PMLA* LXX [Dec. 1955], p. 968), who asserts that "Poems are a sub-class of utterances, included within the larger class of all instances of language use."

2. Michael A. K. Halliday, "The Linguistic Study of Literary Texts," *Proceedings of the Ninth International Congress of Linguistics,* ed. H. G. Lunt (The Hague, 1964), p. 302.

3. Halliday, pp. 305–07.

4. René Wellek ("Closing Statement," in *Style in Language,* ed. T. A. Sebeok [New York, 1960], pp. 417–18) puts the matter incisively: "Statistical frequency necessarily ignores the crucial aesthetic problem, the use of a device in its context. No single stylistic device ... is invariable: it is always changed by its particular context ... often the most commonplace, the most normal, linguistic elements are the constituents of literary structure. A literary stylistics will concentrate on the aesthetic purpose of every linguistic device, the way it serves a totality. . . ."

5. Roger Fowler, "Linguistics, Stylistics; Criticism?" *Lingua* XVI (1966), pp. 153–65; "Linguistic Theory and the Study of Literature," in *Essays on Style and Language,* ed. R. Fowler (London, 1966), pp. 1–28. Henceforth, I will refer to these essays as *"Lingua"* and *"Essays."*

Fowler's temperateness represents a great change from the sanguinity of Harold Whitehall, who, in 1951, suggested that with the advent of structural linguistics a new era in literary criticism had dawned. See Whitehall, "From Linguistics to Criticism," *Kenyon Review* XVIII (Summer 1956), p. 415. The first section of this essay appeared as a review of Trager and Smith's *An Outline of English Structure* in the Autumn 1951 issue of the *Kenyon Review.*

6. *Lingua,* p. 155.

7. *Essays,* p. 27: "Linguistics is just one form of training in close reading, and linguists—especially those whose studies have been in a language with a great literature—may be expected to be especially perceptive of the way language works in a literary text."

8. *Lingua,* pp. 159–60.

9. Fowler remarks (*Essays,* p. 10): "It is unlikely that any formal feature, or set of features, can be found, the presence or absence of which will unequivocally identify literature. Put another way, there is probably no absolute formal distinction between literature and non-literature. . . . This conclusion must be of prime importance to the linguist, for it relieves him of the necessity of making special assumptions about the nature of literary form." As I try to show further on, Fowler's conclusion does not follow. That is, if the *language* of literature is not distinctive then the linguist can only do linguistics. But it does not follow that *literature* does not have a distinctive form. Fowler is assuming that the only distinctive feature possible in literature is a linguistic one.

10. *Lingua,* p. 162.

11. *Lingua,* pp. 163–64.

12. *Essays,* p. 21.

13. Alphonse G. Juilland, Review of *L'Epoque Réaliste; Première Partie; Fin du Romantisme et Parnasse,* by Charles Bruneau, in *Essays on the Language of Literature,* ed. Seymour Chatman and Samuel R. Levin (Boston, 1967), pp. 376–77. Juilland remarks (p. 382) that "the literary act is something more than a language act pure and simple; it is a language act invested with an extra dimension. Since this 'literary dimension' has not yet been defined, or even identified, some might doubt its reality. It will suffice to remind them that, materially, the language act too coincides with the acoustic act . . . and this does not prevent it from being something more than an acoustic act pure and simple. . . ."

14. Cleanth Brooks, "The Language of Paradox," in *The Well Wrought Urn* (New York: Harvest Books, 1947), p. 5.

15. Jan Mukarovsky, "Standard Language and Poetic Language," in *A Prague School Reader on Esthetics, Literary Structure, and Style,* ed. Paul L. Garvin (Washington, D.C., 1964), pp. 17–30.

16. Ibid., p. 18.

17. Ibid., p. 19.

18. Ibid.

19. The quoted words are Roman Jakobson's ("Linguistics and Poetics," in Sebeok [see note 4 above], p. 356).

20. For several ideas in this section, I am indebted to an unpublished paper by Richard Ohmann, "Speech Acts and the Definition of Literature."

CHAPTER THREE

THE PSYCHOLOGY OF LITERARY FORM

WE HAVE BEEN considering poetry from the point of view of its maker. The poet uses words mimetically, to make images and symbols, to make a certain kind of play or novel or lyric, which itself imitates a distinctive kind of human action. Turning now to the reader or auditor, we may ask how such an object produces its distinctive effect upon him. We know that he does not respond merely to the words of the poem, that he responds rather to the human action which the poem imitates. This action is more or less adequately "actualized" in the reader.[1] But just how this comes about is a matter of continuing dispute among critics. It is a matter of considerable importance, for one's view of this process affects one's view of the nature of literature and of the proper methods and aims of criticism.

Aristotle's doctrine of catharsis is an attempt to explain this process. But in the *Poetics* we do not have a doctrine, strictly speaking. We have only the word, which Aristotle never refers to after its unique occurrence in Chapter VI. It is Aristotle's commentators who have given us the doctrine, or, rather, the several doctrines explaining what Aristotle meant. These interpretations usually depend upon Aristotle's discussion of education in the Eighth Book of the *Politics,* where he uses the term in connection with a kind of *mousike* designed for the uncultivated, those given to excessive emotion.[2] Now whether we take *catharsis* to involve a purgative or a purifying process—the doctrine remains unsatisfactory; for it merely substitutes one metaphor for another. *How,* exactly, can a play "purify" or "purge" our emotions? That is what we want to know, and the doctrine of catharsis, to my mind at any rate, evades the real issue: It fails to account for our actual experience of tragedy. An explanation of that experience—how it is caused and how it is structured—is, however, implicit in the *Poetics,* and to this I now turn.[3]

I

I begin with three basic Aristotelian ideas: (1) tragedy is an imitation of human action, (2) tragedy arouses pity and fear, and (3) tragedy produces the pleasure proper to it.

We must not, says Aristotle, "demand of tragedy any and every kind of pleasure, but only that which is proper to it . . . . that which comes from pity and fear . . ." In the *Rhetoric* (ii.5.1382a), fear is further defined as

> a pain or disturbance arising from a mental image of impending evil of a destructive or painful sort . . . men do not fear all evils . . . but only such as mean great pain or ruin, and these only when they appear to be . . . imminent . . . Speaking generally, we may say that those things make us fear which when they befall, or threaten, others, make us pity.
>
> (Trans. W. R. Roberts)

Now if we accept this description of fear, we are faced with two problems. First: if fear is a painful emotion, how can tragedy, which arouses such an emotion, afford us pleasure? Secondly: if fear is occasioned by *one's own* expectation of evil, how can fear be aroused in us when we, as spectators of a play, are *not* threatened? Let us defer a consideration of the first problem until we deal with pity (the same problem arises then) and attempt to solve the second problem now.

If we feel fear only when we ourselves are threatened by some evil, and if, as spectators of a tragedy, we *do* feel fear, then it seems to follow inescapably that we must put ourselves into the role of the protagonist—he who is threatened and has cause to fear. This process is not easy to describe; it is not merely an extension of sympathy, nor is it what one school of aesthetics calls empathy. As we watch a performance of *Oedipus Rex,* we do not merely "feel with" Oedipus or enter into his feelings. We imaginatively identify ourselves with him, project ourselves into his fictive being. To say that we become Oedipus is, of course, absurd; we are ourselves. Yet we must "become" him in some sense, for it is not only Oedipus who is threatened; we are threatened too.

This capacity of the human mind, though difficult to analyze and define, seems to me operative in many of the activities of human life. It is involved, I think, in any successful attempt we make to fully comprehend another person's situation. It is involved in human love. It would seem to be a capacity possessed *par excellence* by the successful dramatist or poet.[4] In the social psychology of George Herbert Mead, it is used to account for the genesis of the self in human society.[5]

Identification will not, however, help us to account for the arousal of pity in tragedy. For although pity, like fear, is a painful emotion, it is, unlike fear, felt *for someone else*. We pity those we know well, says Aristotle (*Rhetoric* ii.8.1386a), "so long as they are not too closely allied to us. In the latter case, we have the same feeling as if we ourselves were threatened." It would seem, then, that the spectator's very self-identification with the protagonist will prevent his feeling pity for him; for to feel pity, the spectator must "stand apart from" the protagonist. Yet Aristotle tells us that tragedy arouses both pity *and* fear.

To account for this we shall need to modify our previous analysis. We must conclude that the spectator only *partially* identifies himself with the protagonist, and that he remains partially detached. (Does not the capacity to identify with the other depend on the retention of one's awareness of his otherness?) To the degree that he identifies himslf with the protagonist, the spectator fears the evil that threatens them both; to the degree that he remains detached, the spectator observes ruin come upon the protagonist and pities him. Only thus can the spectator pity and fear simultaneously. What we have arrived at, it appears, is a combination of two venerable aesthetic theories: the theory of empathy (as qualified above) and the theory of aesthetic distance, each modified by the other.

II

"Why is it," St. Augustine wonders (*Confessions* III.2), "that man desires to be made sad, beholding doleful and tragical things, which yet himself would by no means suffer? Yet he desires as a spectator to feel sorrow at them, and this very sorrow is his pleasure." In the terms of our own inquiry, how can tragedy give us pleasure, if both pity and fear are painful emotions? We can resolve this paradox by developing our previous analysis. But first we need to analyze pleasure itself.

We must insist first of all that the pleasure one gets from art is different in kind from sensual pleasure—even though the senses are "utilized" in all the arts. The pleasure that art produces involves the whole soul, not merely this or that sense faculty. Sensual pleasure, then, need not detain us; but how shall we define pleasure which is not sensual? Our best approach will be to discover its source in real life, for the pleasure of art is not essentially different from that involved in life.

Now in life itself the "lowest" (i.e., least intense and least complex) pleasure results from, or is a concomitant of, simple existence. One is, of course, seldom aware of such pleasure; it is so slight that it usually goes unnoticed—especially during periods of health and security. But during times of peril, when one's existence is threatened, one becomes acutely aware, not only of the desirability of life, but of the pleasure involved in merely being. At such times, misery and pain do not seem really to matter: The only thing that matters is life itself.

If simple existence is the source of the simplest and least intense pleasure, it seems to follow that "higher" (more complex and more intense) pleasure comes about as a result of higher states of existence. And higher states of existence are achieved through *action*, in the sense defined by Fergusson: not outward, physical deeds, but the movement or activity of the soul in any of its modes. It follows, furthermore, that the level of existence achieved through action will depend upon the degree of *order* implicit in it. Since the action is human action, it must be ordered primarily with respect to moral principle.[6] Hence the higher or more complex the principle with respect to which the action is ordered, and the better ordered it is, the higher will be the level of existence achieved. And the greater will be the resultant, or concomitant, pleasure.

What, then, of the emotions? The emotions, I suggest, are simply *signs of action*. The more intense and finely ordered the action engaged in, the more intense will be the emotions. The quality of pleasure will vary in direct proportion to the quality of emotion, or (if you will) to the level of existence that gives rise to it.[7]

Now tragedy is an imitation of human action. And the spectator, by partially identifying himself with the protagonist and by observing the tragic action, *himself* engages in highly ordered and complex action. His pleasure, therefore, should be proportionate to the quality of the tragedy he both witnesses and vicariously engages in. But what of the pain involved in pity and fear?

There is no pain. Since the spectator only partially identifies himself with the protagonist and remains partially detached, he can, and does, fear the evil which seems to threaten them both; but he is at the same time aware that the evil which threatens the protagonist does not really threaten him, that what occurs on the stage is, after all, only on the stage. And the same holds true of pity. Thus the spectator, possessed of this double consciousness, engages in highly-ordered action and feels the consequent emotions and pleasure. *But not the pain.* In real life, pity and fear are painful because they occur while one is facing actual evil. But in watching a tragedy, one has the pleasure which is a concomitant of the action, without the pain. "The delight of tragedy," Dr. Johnson observes, "proceeds from our consciousness of fiction; if we thought murders and treasons real, they would please us no more."

The spectator's partial detachment not only enables him to avoid the pain involved in real-life pity and fear; it enables him also to view the action "from the outside," so to speak, to see it as an ordered and meaningful whole. And this perception, reaching fullness at the close of the play, further enhances the spectator's pleasure.[8]

This process has a countertype in common experience. Everyone, I suppose, has gone through intensely painful experiences. Now while one is going through such an experience, he is so much engaged in it *as* actor that he is incapable of viewing it as a whole, in all its relations and in its full significance. Only as *recalled* does such an experience become really meaningful—and this not merely because of the passage of time. When one recalls such an experience, he makes of it something like a vestigial drama: He patterns the events, attributes motivation, fixes causal and temporal relations. The recaller, moreover, becomes simultaneously both *actor* and *observer*. He relives his experience and at the same time stands apart from himself, viewing his experience as a complete and meaningful whôle. And this is why one's experience—even painful experience—is never so meaningful, so pleasurable, as when it is recalled as part of the past.

A similar process, I suggest, takes place in the spectator of a tragedy—except that in a tragedy the order and meaning are pre-determined by the dramatist. Having engaged in the action of the play, the spectator can, at the close of the play, see that action as a meaningful whole because of his partial detachment. In a famous passage, A. C. Bradley remarks that the spectator of a tragedy "acquiesces" in the terrible events of the play only because he can perceive some sort of moral order underlying them. Yes; and it is precisely his detachment that enables him to see it.

III

The great playwrights of the past have used a number of devices to promote in the spectator that partial detachment which (I have argued) is a necessary condition for the tragic effect. One of the functions of the Chorus in Greek tragedy is to "remove" the spectator, to prevent too close an identification with the protagonist. This function complements that of providing moral and emotional standpoints for the spectator. In Shakespeare's tragedies, in place of a Chorus, we find "choric" characters (Enobarbus, Friar Laurence, Lear's Fool) and, perhaps more important, "choric" scenes, which place the spectator at key moments "outside" the action, and so enable him to see the

action as a meaningful whole. Such a scene is the Willow scene
in *Othello* (IV.iii), where we are given an objective vision of
all the beauty that Othello is soon to destroy. We also get a
poignant sense of what might have been: as we watch Desdemona preparing for bed (she senses that she will die this night)
her mind turns to poor Barbary and her Willow song—and then
to Lodovico.

> *Desd.* This Lodovico is a proper man.
> *Emilia.* A very handsome man.

A fellow Venetian of her own class, Lodovico is just the sort of
man she would have married in the ordinary course of events.
And a moment later we get her solemn banter with Emilia:
"Wouldst thou do such a deed for all the world?" which brilliantly illuminates the goodness that enmeshes them all.

In some tragedies Shakespeare also uses another device. The
hero, especially at the very end, will see himself as an actor in
his own drama. Whether this is to be taken as a trait of character
or not is, I think, open to question. But that it makes for detachment in the spectator seems to me beyond doubt. In the closing
moments of the play, the hero will suddenly stand apart from
himself, see himself as from a perspective beyond his own awareness. The resultant detachment in the spectator intensifies his
pity and sharpens his vision of the whole play. The most notable
instance occurs in *Othello*:

> Then you must speak
> Of one that loved not wisely but too well . . .
>
> (V.ii.342-43)

The effect may be profoundly ironic, as in Brutus':

> My heart doth joy that yet in all my life
> I found no man but he was true to me.
>
> (V.v.34–35)

Which focuses Brutus' self-betrayal and his betrayal by Cassius,
of which he never becomes fully aware—though we do. There is
an even finer irony in Coriolanus':

> If you have writ your annals true, 'tis there,
> That, like an eagle in a dovecote, I

> Flutter'd your Volscians in Corioles.
> Alone I did it.

(V.v.113–16)

It is the only time in the play he boasts, and it is a moment that illuminates his story for us as nothing else could.

The use of verse in tragedy, aside from its virtue as a vehicle of precise eloquence, has this further advantage: It serves, by its formality, to lift the tragic action above the plane of "real life." Many a critic has noted the depressing effect of most modern attempts at tragedy, as contrasted with the exhilaration felt at the close, say, of *King Lear*. The reason for this is not, as some have argued, that modern man has lost his sense of human dignity, but that the modern playwright strives for (and is praised for) the utmost in verisimilitude. His characters speak (usually) a naturalistic and ineloquent prose, and they are on our level morally and socially. His stage is a picture-frame stage with all the naturalistic conventions that go with it. He does not provide any formal means to keep the spectator from too fully identifying himself with the protagonist. As a result, the spectator cannot detach himself sufficiently to perceive whatever meaning the play may possess. And many a modern tragedy is actually painful.

IV

We have been dealing all along with tragedy. But the theory of tragic effect outlined here may be generalized to other literary genres. Aristotle seems to have thought of his discussion of tragedy in the *Poetics* as exemplary and paradigmatic. He starts out to deal with the art of poetry in general and then focuses mainly on the art of tragedy-making. But, as Else points out, the general art "continues to exist and operate *through* the species . . . 'tragedy' (that is, the *art of making* tragedy) actualizes and represents that generic nature *par excellence*."[9]

Our analysis of tragic effect can be extended, if properly qualified, to other literary forms. The different dramatic genres may be distinguished from each other not only, as Aristotle suggests, in terms of the kind of action each imitates, but in terms of the degree of detachment or identification proper to each. Each literary form is an imitation of human action by means of words, and each attains its effect through a psychological process analogous to the one we have outlined for tragedy. The novelist, it seems clear, even the realistic novelist, does not face the same difficulties in achieving detachment as does the realistic dramatist. For the novel is "reading matter"; it does not present its action with the immediacy—auditory and visual—of the drama. The lyric poem, because of its lack of plot and character, because of its more obvious "formality," involves its reader in the least intense identification. And this may account for the lyric's greater utilization of linguistic, rhetorical, and prosodic sources of poetic power.

The most useful feature of this theory of poetic effect—what makes it appear more adequate to our actual experience of poetry than other such theories—is that it enables us to account for both the cognitive and the affective elements in our response. These elements—in our response and in the work—are, of course, only logically separable; they comprise in actuality a single complex experience. Ordinary life experience is never a matter of pure thought or pure feeling, but is always a combination of both. So, too, in our response to literature, for the work of literature is an imitation of *human* action.

The theory has implications, too, for the methodology of literary criticism. It means that the critic must both begin and end with the work's action: the complex of thought and feeling which the work elicits in him and which is formed *in* the work. This, of course, admits a degree of subjectivity into critical procedure and discourse, but this subjectivity is inescapable and is always present—though it may be masked by an objective-sounding terminology or by a rhetorical strategy of "by-passing" the stage of direct response. This does not mean that the critic lets himself go, that he engages in unbridled impressionism. He is always obliged to check his response against its cause, to analyze the work in order to verify or correct his response. This analysis is itself not wholly "objective": it involves an assessment of the responses of a reader or auditor to their structural causes in the work, an assessment which is imaginative or, in some sense, subjective. The "object" of the critic's labors, in brief, is not the words on the page subjected to cool analysis after the fact of his experience of the work; it is the experience itself—never fully realized, but made as nearly adequate as intelligence, training, and sensibility can make it.

NOTES FOR CHAPTER THREE

1. I assume here and throughout a norm of human nature and human response, a set of common traits possessed by all men, whatever their differences of personality or culture. Unless there exists such a norm (to confine ourselves to our own Western culture), it is difficult to understand how the poet or the critic can communicate with anyone. All critics, I think, assume some kind of norm in the very act of *writing* about literature. Of course each reading, each response, is also unique; but a good reader is aware of those aspects of his response which are purely "personal" and, so far as he can, suppresses them.

2. Aristotle tells us (*Politics* 1342a) that he will explain his use of the term "hereafter when we speak of poetry." But he never keeps his promise.

3. We are focusing on tragic effect, but we are concerned ultimately with poetic effect in general.

4. Or the orator. The *locus classicus* is *Ion* 535 A, where Socrates asks Ion, ". . . does not your spirit seem to take part in the events you narrate, whether they are in Ithaca or Troy or any other place you tell of?" (Jowett trans.)

5. George Herbert Mead, *Mind, Self, and Society* (Chicago, 1934). The following (p. 300) is worth quoting:

To take a distinctively human, that is, self-conscious, social attitude toward another individual, or to become aware of him as such, is to identify yourself sympathetically with him, by taking his attitude toward, and his role in, the given social situation, and by thus responding to that situation implicitly as he does or is about to do explicitly; in essentially the same way you take his attitude toward yourself in gestural conversation with him, and are thus made self-conscious. Human social activities depend very largely upon social co-operation among the human individuals who carry them on, and such co-operation results from the taking by these individuals of social attitudes toward one another. Human society endows the human individual with a mind; and the very social nature of that mind requires him to put himself to some degree in the experiential places of, or to take the attitudes of, the other individuals. . . .

6. By "moral principle" I mean the (usually implicit) principles which guide the choices of the characters, which are inferable from their speeches and acts and which in large measure determine our interpretation of character and plot. These principles need not correspond with our own, but they must be intelligible. (In the lyric, the "choices" are usually incipient or potential; they are, in other words, moral attitudes, revealed by the speaker's thought and feeling about the subject or situation of the poem.)

This is not to say that a play is a moral allegory or that poetry is essentially didactic. It is to say that at all points in a play a character's words and deeds have moral status and that the spectator, in ways that have been shown, participates in this morally informed action. In this sense, moral principle is a part of the *aesthetic* structure of the work, an aspect of its form. It serves to elicit in the spectator a correspondingly formed response. And the work will be better or worse (putting aside its other formal attributes) in proportion as the principles involved are important and valid. The "morality of art" is therefore not "what art teaches" or the proper distribution of good and evil fortune to the virtuous and evil characters. It is a *condition* for meaningful structure and one basis of formal value.

7. Aristotle's analysis of pleasure is profound and incisive. I do not know why commentators on the *Poetics* have virtually ignored it. My own indebtedness to Aristotle will be indicated by the following passages (*Nicomachean Ethics* X.4.1174a–1175a, passim):

> Since every sense is active in relation to its object, and a sense which is in good condition acts perfectly in relation to the most beautiful of its objects . . . it follows that in the case of each sense the best activity is that of the best-conditioned organ in relation to the finest of its objects. And this activity will be most complete and pleasant. For, while there is pleasure in respect of any sense, and in respect of thought and contemplation no less, the most complete is pleasantest, and that of a well-conditioned organ in relation to the worthiest of its objects is the most complete; and the pleasure completes the activity. But the pleasure does not complete it in the same way as the combination of object and sense, both good, just as health and the doctor are not in the same way the cause of a man's being healthy. . . .

Pleasure completes the activity not as the corresponding permanent state does, by its immanence, but as an end which supervenes as the bloom of youth does on those in the flower of their age. . . . pleasure . . . accompanies activity.

One might think that all men desire pleasure because they all aim at life; life is an activity, and each man is active about those things and with those faculties that he loves most. . . . It is with good reason, then that they aim at pleasure, too, since for everyone it completes life, which is desirable.   (Trans. W. D. Ross)

8.   The spectator's response can never be identical with that of the protagonist, for he always remains to some degree detached from the protagonist, always sees beyond the protagonist's vision. The degree of detachment will, of course, vary from play to play.

9.   Else, p. 4.

CHAPTER FOUR

RHYTHM AND METER

WE HAVE DEALT so far with *mimesis* by means of language, the
use of language to make images and symbols which themselves
imitate human action. In this process, as we have seen, there is a
stage at which the thing made resembles what it imitates. Now in
addition to this "representative imitation," there is another kind
of *mimesis* which by-passes the stage of resemblance and "directly" imitates human action. This distinct sort of *mimesis*—we
may call it "rhythmic imitation"—is hinted at in the first chapter of the *Poetics* when Aristotle speaks of rhythm and melody as
media of imitation. And the two kinds of imitation are explicitly
distinguished in Chapter IV, where Aristotle says that there are
two "causes" of poetry in human nature: the instinct for imitation, and the instinct for melody and rhythm.

The notion of rhythmic imitation raises a number of questions.
In what sense is rhythm, which does not resemble anything, imitative? And how does rhythm attain its emotional effect upon us?
As we shall see, these are closely connected questions. Before we
can answer them, however, we must try to find answers to two
prior questions. What is rhythm? And how is it produced? We
shall take up these questions here, deferring the other two to the
next chapter. In order to make our discussion as specific and
concrete as possible, we shall consider only one kind of rhythm,
the rhythm of English verse.

I

In the past, it has been customary for prosodists to describe
the metrical practice of poets and to derive from it a set of prac-

43

tical "rules." No one, so far as I know, has attempted to relate these rules to what might be called the ontology of rhythm. I propose to attempt this, beginning with an inquiry into the nature of rhythm.

If we consider the simplest instance of rhythm in our common experience—let us say the ticking of a clock—we may properly infer the following. First, rhythm involves the repetition or recurrence of similar sensuous contents (here, the ticks). The very idea of recurrence "contains" the idea of similarity: To recur is for similar things to succeed each other. Second, rhythm involves such repetition *in time*. This is also dialectically deducible: What happens *again* happens *after* its prior occurrence. Third, rhythm involves such repetition at regular (equal or proportional) temporal intervals. If we agree that the clock's ticking is an instance of rhythm, I do not see how any of these inferences can be denied—though they need further qualification.

Upon further analysis of our experience, it appears that the rhythm does not inhere in the recurrent ticking as such. The rhythm is felt when the mind perceives, by way of the senses, the temporal relations which are articulated by the recurring sensuous content (ticking, drum beats, syllabic stress). This sensuous "embodiment" is necessary for the expression of these relations—so that the mind may perceive them. Even when imagined, a rhythm is always embodied in some imagined sensuous content. Rhythm, then, is a *psychological* reality: It is felt when the mind perceives certain temporal relations; it exists in the ticking itself only as a potential cause.[1]

It appears, furthermore, that the intervals between recurrences need be only approximately equal or proportional. If, for example, we hasten or delay a particular tick in a series, we may still feel the whole sequence as regular—provided that we do not hasten or delay the particular tick too much. The mind seems capable (up to a point) of perceiving regularity in matter that is not objectively regular, but only approximately so.

The third of our inferences needs the most discussion, for W. K. Wimsatt and Monroe Beardsley, in a 1959 article, have flatly denied that English meter is temporally measured. Our discussion here would be more precise if we first distinguished between rhythm and meter. But since Wimsatt and Beardsley do not make this distinction, we may assume for the moment that these two aspects of verse structure are the same.

Wimsatt and Beardsley's strongest argument runs:

> Meter involves measurement, no doubt, or it can hardly with much meaning be called "meter." But all measurement is not necessarily temporal measurement—even when the things measured occur in a temporal succession. If a person walks along the street hitting every third paling in a fence, he sets up a pattern, but he may or he may not do this in equal lengths of time. Better still, let every third paling be painted red, and we have a pattern which our person does not have to set up for himself but can observe objectively. He will observe or experience this pattern in time but not necessarily in equal lengths of time.[2]

If it is not time which is measured in verse, then what is measured? In a critique of the Wimsatt–Beardsley article, Joseph W. Hendren asks this question and is answered thus: "Syllables, numbers of syllables, are measured—syllables according to stress and slack, so many slacks between each stress."[3] What is measured then is a mathematical quantity, one which makes "a linguistic and intelligible contour." It is difficult to see why any piece of prose arranged in lines of a certain number of syllables would not make such an "intelligible contour." Why should the poet write in verse at all? The view, founded on experience and maintained by theorists since Plato, that rhythm in some way affects the feelings of the listener is apparently rejected. The pattern is "not 'pure cerebration' of course (the mental action is expressed by phonetic utterance in time), but nevertheless not a simply physical pattern, not like drum taps, or walking, or breathing."[4] I do not understand this.

The pattern in the fence is one which the walker can "observe objectively." That last phrase, I believe, is the key to Wimsatt and Beardsley's position. They do not wish to "locate" an aspect of the poem in the reader; they want everything to be objectively there in the poem. But as I have already pointed out, rhythm is a psychological reality in that it takes place in a human being's

consciousness. It is something *felt,* though it is virtually existent
—embodied *in potentia*—in some kind of sensuous material.
Unless one recognizes the psychological status of rhythm, he cannot be made to see its temporal basis. One must *feel* rhythm in
order to talk about it. If one doesn't feel it, if one assumes it to
be an "objective" rather than a psychological reality, logical
argument will hardly be convincing.

The fence analogy actually begs the whole question by imaging
what is essentially a temporal phenomenon as a spatial one.[5] The
person hitting every third paling will set up a pattern corresponding to a metrical one *only if he walks at a steady pace.*
Otherwise, the pattern is a spatial one, and spatial patterns have
nothing to do with rhythm and meter. I think Wimsatt and
Beardsley would find aesthetically invalid such seventeenth-
century experiments with "visual" verse as Herbert's "Easter
Wings" or Dylan Thomas's more recent efforts of that sort.
I think they would agree that language is made of sounds which
occur in time and that it differs from bricks and mortar which
exist in space.[6]

From the fence analogy, Wimsatt and Beardsley draw this
conclusion:

> The measurement of verse is determined by some recurrent lin-
> guistic feature. . . . If we read this recurrence so as to give it
> equal times, this is something we do to it. Maybe we actually do,
> and maybe this is part of our aesthetic satisfaction; still it is not
> a part of linguistic fact which the poet has to recognize and on
> which he has to rely in order to write verses.[7]

The linguistic feature by which most English verse is measured
(that is, all of it except for the few experiments in syllabic or
"quantitative" verse) is stress. But the recurrent stresses do not
measure themselves or numbers of syllables; they measure *time.*
They are a formal means for signalling the temporal relations in
the line. Wimsatt and Beardsley admit that a feature which recurs recurs in time; they are not sure that it recurs in equal
periods. If, however, it does not recur in equal (or approximately equal) times, there is little point to its recurring at all.

Their dubiety, furthermore, as to whether equal timing provides aesthetic satisfaction ought to disqualify their judgments about it.

It is true that giving relatively equal times to the intervals between stresses "is something we do" to the poem. But only in a sense. When we do this, we are simply reading the poem properly, actualizing what is potentially and determinately there in the poem. For equal timing is also something that the *poet* has done to the poem—if he is a good maker of meter and rhythm.[8] Equal timing is not, to be sure, "a part of linguistic fact." But, as Wimsatt and Beardsley are well aware, the poem itself is not, in the sense they use the term, a linguistic fact; it is an aesthetic object. The poem *uses* linguistic fact (words, syllables, stresses) to make an auditory artifact; a structure of sound, occurring in time, conveying to the mind through the ear a distinctive pattern, which (in conjunction with the verbal and poetic meaning with which it co-exists) determinately affects the feelings of the hearer.[9] In English verse this pattern is a temporal pattern, and its name is "rhythm."

II

Wimsatt and Beardsley's misconception of the nature of meter stems in part from their failure to distinguish clearly between meter and rhythm. I have already defined rhythm in a general way. Let me now distinguish it from, and show its relation to, meter.

Ordinarily when we speak of meter we have in mind the series of visual marks with which we "scan" a poem, indicating "feet" and the stressed and unstressed syllables. We thus actualize (visually) for purposes of analysis what is never actually heard in the performance of the poem. This is so because no actual English utterance can correspond exactly with the mathematical perfection of the meter. No matter how normal the utterance, variation in syllable duration and junctural pause will make the sequence of *actual* stresses diverge from the ideal precision of the meter.

But if the meter is never actually heard, how do we know of its existence and its form? First of all, we read the poem and try to understand its words and sentences. Then we go on to an understanding of the poem's meaning as a poem. Once we have arrived at this stage of understanding, we can depend on our habitual knowledge of the way English *sounds,* our intuitive knowledge of what the linguist calls its "prosodic features," to guide us to an inference of the meter. Or, to put it more simply: Once we know the meaning of an utterance, we can tell how to pronounce it. Once we know the meaning of a verse line, we can tell the relative intensity of stress on its syllables. If there *is* a pattern of stresses in the poem, we can then determine its form. (A knowledge of traditional English verse, of course, makes everything much easier.) For example: in the line "Shall I compare thee to a summer's day," we note that every second syllable is stressed more heavily than the one preceding it. We detect this pattern because we know where stresses go on English polysyllables and in an English sentence of this form and meaning. In a different context the pattern might be different, but then the meaning would be different, too. Which is to say that stress is phonemic in English: just as meaning determines stress pattern in ordinary speech, it determines the more formal stress pattern in verse—though it is not the only determinant of this pattern.

A metrical pattern, once it is begun, tends to "impose" itself on succeeding lines. The cause of this is the tendency of the mind to develop and repeat an incipient pattern—in the case of meter, a temporal pattern. When, for example, we come to the words *thee to* in the line I have quoted, even though in ordinary speech the difference between their stresses may be unnoticeable, in the metrical context we will increase the stress on *to* in order to maintain the pattern of which we have become aware.[10] These are the processes by which we infer the *norm* of the line. This norm is the meter: it exists in the mind of the reader (as in the mind of the poet), and though it does not have physical being, it does exist in a determinate form.

We infer the meter of a poem from the words of the poem considered as sound (the sound being a function of meaning).

This sound is differentiated in many ways, but for the purpose of ascertaining the meter of most English verse we attend only to stress. (We attend to syllables, too, but only in a secondary sense: insofar as stress always occurs on, or is located by, a syllable). We perceive differences in stress and note that every second stress (in iambic verse) is stronger than the one preceding it. We perceive, then, a *repetition* or *recurrence* of strong stresses and, between these stresses, *temporal intervals*.

Clearly there *must* be temporal intervals between strong stresses, because the syllables have duration. If we could show that the syllables which make up each foot of an iambic line were equal in duration, we could prove that meter is a pattern of equal temporal intervals. But, though English syllables differ in duration, these differences (except for the grossest) cannot be detected by the ear. They are neither precisely measurable, nor systematic, nor phonemic.

But if English meter is measured by stress rather than by syllable duration, this does not mean that syllables are functionless. They have, in fact, an important function as elements in the traditional "foot structure" of English verse. Since they *have* duration, the syllables make temporal intervals between the repeated heavy stresses in the line. And since their duration does not vary a great deal (i.e., since they vary within definite limits), and since they are "counted" (so many syllables to a foot), they provide *roughly equivalent* intervals between heavy stresses. The mind of the reader does the rest: Given this pattern of roughly equivalent intervals, the mind, with its tendency to discern form in material that does not quite attain it, "creates" the ideal temporal pattern that is the meter.[11]

This is why one cannot prove by mechanical timing that the meter is regularly timed. The actual spoken feet are *not* equal in duration. *But they do not have to be.* The ideal feet of the meter *are* equal in duration, and they can be equal precisely because they are not actual. Meter, then, is an ideal temporal norm, inferred from the actual words of the poem, and existing in the minds of both poet and reader. It is not a rhythm. For though meter involves the recurrence of equal temporal intervals, this pattern is not actualized; it is only implicit in the words which the listener actually hears.

Now if the meter is not the rhythm of a poem, then the rhythm must inhere either in the actual spoken poem or in some relation between the spoken poem and the meter. According to Yvor Winters, "Meter is the arithmetic norm, the purely theoretic structure of the line; rhythm is the controlled departure from that norm."[12] Or, as Winters rephrases his formula (p. 83), rhythm *results from* this departure. We might say, then, that the spoken poem *has* rhythm: its rhythm is a function of both its meter and the departures from the meter which the spoken poem makes. But then we face a kind of dilemma: The meter consists of ideally equal intervals, a norm inferred from the actual words of the poem; on the other hand, the actual words of the poem, precisely because they are actual, cannot create the recurring temporal equivalence which, according to our definition, is required for the creation of rhythm.

A solution to this dilemma is implicit in our previous analysis. Though the intervals between strong stresses are not equal, they do approach equivalence. The foot structure of English verse and the durational limits of English syllables guarantee this. Furthermore, once the *meter* becomes established, it serves as a continuing norm of expectation, making the performance tend toward equivalence. Thus, though the duration of syllables and feet will vary, a proper reading will tend to adjust these variations with periods of silence (like rests in music), so as to make the actual line approach the ideal equivalence of the meter. (The actual line can never, of course, reach such ideal equivalence.)

The rhythm of a poem, then, consists of the perceived relation between: (1) the recurring, approximately equal, temporal units articulated by the actual stresses, syllables and silences of the poem, and (2) the meter—the ideal temporal pattern inferred from the actual poem, but which exists only intersubjectively. In psychological terms, the rhythm involves what has been called "double audition." The listener is simultaneously aware of the actual sound of the poem *and* of its meter, which is "heard" by the mind's ear. If the listener is aware of both the actual and the ideal, it follows that he is also aware of discrepancies between them and feels these discrepancies (Winters' "departures") as more or less significant.[13]

In the light of this analysis, we can see, I think, what is wrong with the prosodic theories of both "timers" and "counters"; we can see also that there is some truth in both positions. The timer tries to impose on English a classical metrical system which English cannot, by its very nature, receive. He usually rejects stress as a structural element in English meter and conceives the line in terms of long and short syllables, which in combination comprise "quantitative" feet. The theory has the advantage of recognizing the temporal nature of English verse; but it fails to take account of the nature of the language out of which English verse is made. Syllable duration, as we noted earlier, is neither systematic nor phonemic in English. It cannot, therefore, serve as a "measure" for English meter. The arrangement of syllables "by ear" is, of course, a source of beauty in much English verse; it helps to produce the extraordinary texture of much of Campion. But even in Campion, the structural basis of meter and rhythm is not syllabic duration, but stress. That is a necessity imposed by the nature of the language.

The counters, on the other hand, though they recognize the primary importance of stress, ordinarily fail to see the function of stress *as a temporal signal*. Instead of conceiving of verse as a temporal structure, they conceive of it, rather, as a spatial or "intelligible" pattern. An adequate theory of English prosody must take into account *both* the primary importance of stress and the temporal nature of rhythm. The theory I have elucidated tries to do just that.

III

I should like now to examine, in the light of this theory, some of the traditional "rules" of English versification. These "permissible variations" and practical precepts, developed "by ear" by a long line of English poets, are, I think, rarely violated without damaging the rhythm of a poem. Yet, at first glance, the commonly accepted variations seem to upset the temporal order of the line and so impugn the theory outlined above. If the theory is sound, it ought to be able to explain these variations, which have a kind of empirical validity.

The most common variation in iambic verse is the substitution of a trochee for an iamb in the first foot. Here are examples:

When to/ the séssions of sweet silent thought

Fóllow/ your sáint, follow with accents sweet

Sée how/ the órient dew

If the strong stresses signal the temporal intervals of the line, will not the displacement of the initial strong stress make the first interval grossly unequal to those in the rest of the line? Many poets have felt that it does not. And if we listen closely, we perceive that we actually *do* maintain approximately equal time throughout the line—in spite of the initial substitution.

In performing the Shakespeare line, we make the interval between the stresses on *When* and *ses* roughly equal to that between strong stresses in the rest of the line. The two intermediate syllables (*to the*) are hurried just enough to make this possible. An initial substitution of this sort may be explained temporally thus.

When tŏ/ thĕ sés/ =∧When/ tŏ thĕ sés/

What happens is that we get the equivalent of an anapest substitution in the second foot; as in other anapest substitutions, the foot's duration approximates that of an iamb, the two light syllables being roughly equal to the single light syllable of an iamb. The first foot "becomes" a defective one in which the time of the dropped light syllable is taken up by silence. This variation thus maintains the temporal measure of the line.

Temporal analysis of inversions *within* the line reveals a similar process. Consider the following lines.

Follow/your sáint,/∧fóllow/with ac/cents sweet

When wee/are thére;/∧hére on/this low/ly ground

Where riv/ers smooth/est rún,/∧deép are/the fords

In each case—the third foot in the first two lines, the fourth foot in the third—the inversion follows a "heavy" pause. We can see now why this is necessary: The pause provides the interval needed to make the time between the stress on *saint* (in the Campion line) and that on *fol* equivalent to that between heavy stresses in the rest of the line. Again, the light syllable *low* and *with* are equivalent to the light syllables of an anapest, making the interval roughly equal to the others.

The rhythmic necessity for a pause before an inversion within the line is most obvious in those lines where a pause is not provided by syntax. In such cases, we must "insert" an unnatural pause and so wrench normal speech pattern—either that or we destroy the rhythm of the line. This line (from Donne's "Twickenham Garden"),

> And can convert manna to gall,

should, according to expectations set up early in the poem, be an iambic tetrameter. But because the inversion of the third foot does not follow a pause, we must read the line as a trimeter:

> Aňd cán/cŏnvĕrt mán/nă tŏ gáll.

If our sense of the meter is strong enough, we may insert a pause after *convert;* meter and rhythm then remain intact, but the normal speech pattern is distorted:

> Aňd cán/cŏnvért/ₐmánnă/tŏ gáll.

The most consistently honored rule about inversion is that it may not occur in the last foot. We might suppose that, if a pause precedes it, such an inversion ought to be as acceptable as any other. Yet not only are such inversions very rare in English verse; where they do occur, we find no preceding pause. In Keats's line— "Bright star, would I were steadfast as thou art"—the inversion of the last foot demanded by the sense is overridden by the force of the meter. So that we get a rhythmically sound line, but one in which natural stressing (i.e., stressing according to meaning) is wrenched. In other cases the stressing demanded by the sense is too emphatic to be overridden—as in this line of Vaughan's:

Năy, háth/nŏt só/mŭch wít/ăs sóme/stónes hăve.

The final foot must be inverted, and this results in a grossly unequal interval between the last two strong stresses. The duration
of the whole line, signalled by the last strong stress, is also short-
ened, so that it departs from the duration of the other lines. The
traditional rule is again justified by temporal analysis.

   The only exception I know to this rule occurs in this line of
Vaughan's:

Thăt hé/hăth qúite/fŏrgót/hów tŏ/gó thĕre.

At first glance, this appears to be similar to the previous line in
its violation of meter and rhythm. On close analysis, however,
we discover that no such violation occurs. For the fourth foot is
also inverted, and *a pause occurs before the fourth foot*. This
has the effect of equalizing, not only the fourth foot, but the final
foot as well. To indicate the line's temporal structure, we might
scan it thus:

Thăt hé/hăth qúite/fŏrgót/ʌ hów/tŏ gó/thĕre.

In the fourth foot the dropped light syllable is made up by a
pause, the fifth foot is not inverted, and we get a common feminine ending. (In terms of conventional scansion, the fifth foot *is*
inverted.)

   My final example is this line from Donne's *Elegy X:*

Sŏ, íf/Ĭ dréame/Ĭ háve/yŏu, Í/háve yŏu.

A perusal of the whole poem shows that heavy stress must come
on the second *have* rather than on the second *you*. The resultant
shortening of the final interval and of the duration of the whole
line obviously impairs its rhythm. Arnold Stein finds Donne's
ineptness here an occasion for implicit praise. The reader, according to Stein, "tries out" all possibilities of stressing and perceives all the ambiguities so suggested. "And so . . . all of the
possibilities are contained in the scansion the ear at last elects.
The result is a kind of ambiguous hovering that includes (in the
pyrrhic-spondee of the last four syllables) both the reality of
possession and the reality of identity, and includes them in their
dynamic relationship to each other."[14]

This is fascinating, but it is also, I think, quite wrong. As we have seen earlier, the meaning of a poem determines the stressing of its lines. Taken in context, the line is not ambiguous in meaning; and it is wrong to "impose" ambiguity on it by devising for it the stress pattern Stein proposes.[15] Stein also does not seem to understand the principle of relative stress: The stressed syllable in iambic verse is determined *within* the foot. (It is this principle which makes English iambic verse capable of such great variety within normal metrical contexts. It also makes the pyrrhic-spondee pattern virtually impossible.) Stein's assumption, finally, that stress pattern can serve as a kind of metaphor is clearly fallacious. The relation between rhythm and meaning, i.e., how rhythm qualifies or conveys meaning, is an obscure one (I take it up in the next chapter). But this much is clear: the relation between rhythm and meaning in verse is *not* the same as that between stress pattern and meaning in ordinary speech. Stein confuses the phonemic status of stress with the use to which it is put in creating rhythm, which is an aesthetic, not a linguistic, entity.

IV

I have not meant to suggest, by these exercises in temporal analysis, that the manifold complexities of English verse rhythm may be so simply accounted for. I have been trying to establish the basic principles of English verse; in most good verse there are rhythmic complexities which I have not begun to suggest. In these lines,

> When to the sessions of sweet silent thought
> I summon up remembrance of things past,

a knowledge that the intervals between strong stresses are approximately equal, that the meter and rhythm are distinct and must be understood in temporal terms—this only helps us to establish the meter and "ground rhythm" of the poem. Only after we have grasped the meaning and rhythm of the whole poem can we "hear" and so be able to perform the poem properly. The second line seems, at first glance, quite regular:

> I súm/mon úp/remém/brance óf/things pást.

But if we listen carefully, we will find that, superimposed on this pattern and simultaneous with it, there is another one:

I súmmon up/remémbrance/of things pást.

The line has a tri-partite structure, its three parts coincident with the three word groups which compose it; and this secondary pattern, it seems, is also composed of roughly equivalent intervals. In temporal terms, then, the line has a ground pattern of five, and a secondary pattern of three, intervals. This sort of complexity may be found in most good verse. Though we may not be conscious of it, it accounts for our sense of rhythmic beauty in verse which, according to conventional scansion, may appear quite ordinary. The rhythmic complexity is there, however, in somewhat the way overtones are present in music.

NOTES FOR CHAPTER FOUR

1. That rhythm does not inhere in the sensuous content as such is cogently argued by D. W. Prall (*Aesthetic Judgment,* [New York, 1929], pp. 144–45): "... rhythm is felt rather than seen or heard. A blind man may keep time silently with slight motions of his hands or feet or head; or feel his own pulses within the measured pattern of their beat. And if we often connect the notion of rhythm with seen movements and heard sounds, we cannot afford to forget that what is seen is not the rhythm itself, but the content that is occurring rhythmically. ... The rhythm has to do with the order and rate and manner of their occurrence to perception, not ... with the quality of the tones themselves, which is definitely tonal and timeless. A deaf man watching the conductor's baton, may be made to feel the identical rhythm that is felt and distinguished as formal pattern by a blind man listening to the sounds ... of the orchestra. Obviously, then, rhythm is neither sound quality nor color quality, but an order established and marked in the occurrence of these."

2. "The Concept of Meter: An Exercise in Abstraction," *PMLA* LXXIV (December, 1959), p. 590.

3. Joseph W. Hendren, W. K. Wimsatt, Jr., and Monroe C. Beardsley, "A Word for Rhythm and a Word for Meter," *PMLA* LXVI (June, 1961), p. 307.

4. Ibid.

5. I leave out of account Hendren's experiment with an actual situation of this sort, which undercuts Wimsatt and Beardsley's whole argument. See "A Word for Rhythm," p. 304.

6. Rhythm may, of course, be involved in the spatial arts. But when we say that a painting has rhythm, what we mean (unless we are using a rather dubious metaphor) is that the eye of the beholder moves *in time* over regularly recurring elements in the painting and that the beholder feels this recurrence as a timed pattern. What is involved, then, is a temporal pattern, not a spatial one. See Prall, p. 150. See also F. De Saussure, *Course in General Linguistics* (New York, 1959), p. 70: "In contrast to visual signifiers (nautical signals, etc.) which can offer simultaneous groupings in several dimensions, auditory signifiers have at their command only the dimension of time; their elements are presented in time; they form a chain. This feature becomes readily apparent when they are represented in writing and the spatial line of graphic marks is substituted for succession in time."

7. "The Concept of Meter," p. 590.

8. That no two performances are exactly alike does not disprove the temporal basis of English verse. Performances may be simply bad. But even good ones will vary from each other. A solution to this problem must wait on the distinction between meter and rhythm made below. For now, two points are in order. First, temporal equivalence is never absolute and does not need to be, for rhythm is a psychological, not a physical, phenomenon. Second, good performances will never vary so much as to destroy *the basic time scheme* of a poem. As Hendren puts it ("A Word for Rhythm," p. 301): "Rhythm . . . is not damaged by pauses or expressive shifts of speed, either slow or sudden. Even in . . . music this is true. Different singers vary the duration of syllables, but no competent singer ever violates a time signature."

9. Strictly speaking, the senses do not perceive rhythm—even though rhythm becomes known *through* the senses. Sense perception is always immediate: We perceive this or that sound *now*, and our perceiving it is not in itself a perception of rhythm. Of course, the listener "hears" rhythm. But such a statement is ambiguous. Since the ear has no memory, the listener must call upon some power other than the sense of hearing in order to perceive a pattern extended in time. This may be why Aristotle says that rhythm and melody possess "moral character" as opposed to the objects of the other senses.

10. This tendency of meter to "enforce" the stressing of syllables which would not be stressed in ordinary speech is most noticeable in anapestic meters, making such meters nearly useless for good verse. The rhythm of anapestic verse is "enslaved" by the meter, the

stresses being inflexibly heavy, the intervals approaching mechanical and inexpressive equivalence.

11. The relation between the abstract meter and the spoken words of the poem is analogous to that between Plato's Ideas and their images. The Ideas are ideal and perfect, but we know them by way of their imperfect imitations in the actual world.

12. *The Function of Criticism* (Denver, 1957), p. 82. For an explanation of the relation of meter and rhythm in music, see Igor Stravinski, *Poetics of Music* (New York: Vintage Books, 1956), pp. 29–30.

13. Many critics (Winters among them) believe that rhythm involves a tension between the undifferentiated "beat" of the meter and the varying intensities of the spoken stresses. But this is not a rhythmic (i.e., a temporal) matter. The variation of stress that comes into English verse with Sidney is a source of beauty, but it is rhythmically significant only as it may be used to signal secondary temporal patterns. As Prall says (p. 145): ". . . rhythm is neither sound quality nor color quality, but an order established and marked in the occurrence of these." In English verse this order is a temporal one.

14. Arnold Stein, "Donne's Prosody," *Kenyon Review* XVIII (Summer, 1956), p. 440.

15. See my interpretation of *Elegy X* in *Explicator XIX* (June, 1961), Item 67.

CHAPTER FIVE

RHYTHM AND MEANING

EQUIPPED WITH A definition of rhythm and some understanding
of how it is produced in English verse, we are prepared to tackle
the question we have so far deferred: How does rhythm attain
its effect upon the human soul? Or, to put it differently, what
exactly is the relation between rhythm and meaning?[1] Our answer
will in part depend on an understanding of the Aristotelian notion
that rhythm is, in some sense, imitative.

I

Critics seldom theorize about the relation between rhythm and
meaning, but they assume certain theories whenever they attempt
to analyze particular rhythmic effects. Brooks and Warren, for
example, tell us that the rhythm of Yeats' line—"Speech after
long silence; it is right"—

> supports with dramatic appropriateness, the effect of informal
> conversation. . . . *Speech* is accented emphatically, as it should
> be for dramatic reasons: the abrupt beginning is appropriate to
> the idea of speech suddenly breaking upon silence. . . . the
> emphasis on *long* [is] greater than it would otherwise be; and
> this heavy emphasis on *long* fortifies the meaning of the word.[2]

Two distinct theories are implicit here. The appeal to dramatic
appropriateness implies that rhythm in verse works its effect by
imitating the natural speech rhythm of a speaker, thus re-creating
the fictive situation and the speaker's feeling and attitude. The
rest of the passage implies a second theory: that rhythm is equivalent to stress pattern and that the poet, by controlling stress
intensity and arrangement, controls meaning. Let us call the first

59

theory "the imitative theory," the second, "the rhetorical stress theory."

Now with regard to the second theory, though stress intensity and arrangement are always related to meaning in English, this relation is a different one from the relation between rhythm and meaning. What makes the matter confusing is that stress is *also* used to make meter and rhythm. What we are trying now to discover is the relation between *rhythm* and meaning— not that between *stress* and meaning—about which linguistics, especially American linguistics, has told us a great deal. This sentence, for example, has three different meanings, depending upon stress arrangements:

> I *won't* go home. ("Under no circumstances will I go home.")
> *I* won't go home. ("Others may go home, but I won't.")
> I won't go *home*. ("I may go somewhere, but I won't go home.")

In a poem, of course, the arrangement and intensity of stress is a matter of interpretation; to perform properly, we must first know the meaning of the poem. Whereas in ordinary speech, we *indicate* meaning by stress pattern and the other suprasegmentals that we impose on our utterances. It is clear, I think, that the rhetorical stress theory simply confuses this process with the process by which rhythm attains its effect. Rhythm is not a stress pattern merely—though it is articulated by stress; it is, rather, a *temporal* pattern of the sort I have tried to describe.[3]

The imitative theory raises a number of troublesome questions. Is rhythm imitative in the same way and in the same sense that speech and color and shape are imitative? If so, what exactly does it imitate? Both Plato and Aristotle regard rhythm as one of the media of imitation, on a par with speech and color and shape. We can readily see how drama and painting imitate: The drama resembles—"re-creates"—the men-doing-things of which it is an imitation; the painting *looks* like the scene or person it depicts. In the case of rhythm, however, we can find no such resemblance. Rhythm, it would seem, can only imitate something else which is rhythmic.

According to Plato and Aristotle, rhythm and melody imitate, not sensuously perceivable things or physical acts, but *inner* realities—character, feelings, states or activities of the soul. Our own experience supports such a view: Rhythm does seem to express, or elicit in us, such inner realities. Yet where is the resemblance which underlies the idea of imitation? Rhythm is a temporal pattern; character, feeling, etc. are never outwardly manifest and would seem, therefore, to be inimitable. What does a feeling look like or sound like?

We know our own feelings because we directly intuit them. We know about them in others *only by way of signs:* gestures, facial expressions, actions, speech. Such signs reveal feeling; they are not feeling as such. They do not *imitate* feeling; they are *signs* of feeling. Drama and painting express character, feeling, the activity of the soul *indirectly*. That is, the dramatist and painter *imitate* the natural signs of these inner realities. They cannot directly imitate these inner realities. Rather, they create fictive natural signs which signify the inner realities. Thus there is resemblance in such imitating, but the resemblance is between the fictive signs and the natural signs and not between the signs and what they signify. Rhythm and melody, on the other hand, do not make use of natural signs. Rather, they *directly* express what drama and painting indirectly express. One stage of the "imitative" process is, as it were, short-circuited. Perhaps this is what Aristotle means when he says that the musical arts are more imitative than the others.[1]

How exactly do rhythm and melody express character, feeling, etc.? There is in us, says Aristotle (*Politics* VIII.v.1340b), "a sort of affinity to musical modes and rhythms, which makes some philosophers say that the soul is a tuning. . . ." Rhythm and melody, says Plato (*Republic* III.401), "find their way into the secret places of the soul, on which they mightily fasten, bearing grace in their movements, and making the soul graceful . . . or ungraceful. . . ." These passages suggest a sense in which rhythm may be said to be imitative. Rhythm is a temporal pattern articulated by some sensuous content recurring in time. Now the soul also exists and "moves" in time. We may say, then, that rhythm, so far as it expresses character, feeling, the activity of the soul, *corresponds* with (directly imitates) the movement of the soul. The affinity Aristotle speaks of depends upon the modal correspondence of rhythm and the soul's activity: Both attain their particular forms through the discriminate pattern of their movement in time. We might say, then, that the activity of the soul is rhythmic, even though its "rhythms" are not overt. The rhythm of verse, so far as it is effective, elicits in the soul of the listener the inner rhythms to which it corresponds, or which, in the sense defined, it imitates.[5]

Now if rhythm *directly* imitates feeling, then the "imitative" theory of Brooks and Warren is mistaken to this extent: It assumes that the object of imitation is "natural" speech, i.e., actual, casual, everyday, practical speech. But this view is clearly absurd. For the rhythm of verse is obviously "artificial"—carefully wrought, a product of deliberate art; whereas the rhythm of ordinary speech is very loose and unpremeditated. So that the rhythm of verse cannot be said to imitate the rhythm of casual speech—or even that of "artistic" prose. No one speaks in verse—except the poet or the actor. And if the aim of the poet were to imitate the rhythm of natural speech, he ought to abandon verse altogether in favor of exact transcriptions of actual conversation.

One source of confusion about this point is the slipperiness of the term "natural." All verse, in one sense, is composed of "natural" speech in that it must use the normal syntactic and grammatical rules of the language. But the rhythm of verse is something "super-imposed" on the language. To say this about the rhythm of a poem is but to say what we usually take for granted about the poem itself: that it is an artifact. If, indeed, the poem is to be understood as a poem, the reader must be aware of its being an artifact, and one clue to this is its "artificial" rhythm. To deny this is to fall into the fallacy of imitative form, the notion that a work of art takes (or ought to take) its form from the object which it imitates.

There is only one (special) way in which rhythm can be imitative in the sense of resembling some outwardly manifest object or activity. I am thinking of the rare instance when verse rhythm "sounds like" what the verse is describing—a form of onomatopoeia. Arnold's famous lines are a good example:

Listen! you hear the grating roar
Of pebbles which the waves draw back, and fling,
At their return, up the high strand,
Begin, and cease, and then again begin,
With tremulous cadence slow, and bring
The eternal note of sadness in.

From the second through the fifth line, the rhythm of the verse unquestionably resembles the rhythmic movement of the sea at the seashore. This is possible because what is imitated is itself a rhythmic phenomenon. Yet even here I would insist that the rhythm of Arnold's poem *primarily* expresses—directly imitates—the human feeling which is the real burden of the poem.

Assuming that rhythm expresses feeling in this way, we are faced with two problems as critics of poetry: (1) how are we going to describe rhythm, and (2) how are we going to explain the relation of particular rhythms to the meaning of the poems in which they inhere? With regard to the first problem, we must recognize that, although we have a useful system for describing meter, we possess no systematic notation for describing rhythm. We do, however, have a way of conveying a poem's rhythm to others. If we can scan properly, if we understand the principles of English prosody, if we have trained ears and disciplined voices, we can give a poem precise audible reading. This is really the best "description" possible of a poem's rhythm—just as the best description of a piece of music is a good performance. This is not the place to explain in detail the sort of performance I have in mind. I may say, however, that it should be neither so "unnatural" (or so emphatic of the meter) as to wrench the normal stress patterns of the language, nor so "natural" (or so dramatic) as to destroy a sense of the meter: a reading, in short, that pays tribute to both components of the rhythm and so conveys it with precision.[6]

How are we to explain the relation of this rhythm to the meaning of the poem in which it inheres? I. A. Richards doubts that we can ever do this with the degree of precision which would make it worth doing, and one is inclined, all things considered, to agree with him.[7] Yet if this relation can be *felt* in all good poems (as Richards concedes), it ought to be explicable—not, to be sure, with the nicety which Richards would like—but with whatever accuracy the resources of language and our own sensibilities permit. We can understand why great precision is unattainable: Rhythm expresses what is inexpressible by other means. This is why good audible reading is so important: Since we can describe rhythmic effects only in general, we are obliged to make them *audible* in as precise a manner as possible.

II

Let me attempt to illustrate both the possibilities and limitations of rhythmic analysis. My first text is Hopkins' "Inversnaid," a poem fairly simple and emphatic in thought and feeling, and so an easier case for analysis than most other good poems.

This dárksome búrn, hórseback brówn,

His róllrock híghroad róaring dówn,

In cóop and in cómb the fléece of his fóam

Flútes and lów to the láke falls hóme.

A windpuff-bonnet of fawn-froth
Turns and twindles over the broth
Of a pool so pitchblack, fell-frowning,
It rounds and rounds Despair to drowning.

Degged with dew, dappled with dew
Are the groins of the braes that the brook treads through,
Wiry heathpacks, flitches of fern,
And the beadbonny ash that sits over the burn.

What would the world be, once bereft
Of wet and wildness? Let them be left,
O let them be left, wildness and wet;
Long live the weeds and the wilderness yet.

The meter here is accentual, a rare modern instance of the alliterative native meter of the late Middle Ages. The stresses are pointed by alliteration and are very heavy, making for a palpably isochronic pattern. There is a regular midline caesura. Variation is achieved by way of pauses, the occasional juxtaposition of stresses (as in line five: "fáwn-fróth"), and variation in the number of syllables between stresses. The resultant rhythm is at once very emphatic and uncomplicated. So far as it can be abstracted from the meaning of the words in which it inheres, it expresses joyous, unrestrained excitement.

The feeling I have attributed to the rhythm may, of course, be largely an effect of the meaning; its connection with the rhythm may be illusory. The danger of such an "illusion" is always present in this sort of analysis simply because the rhythm *cannot* actually be separated from the particular words in which it inheres. In any case, the feeling I have attributed to the rhythm of Hopkins' poem is really *a quite general class of feeling*. In order to define it more precisely, it will be necessary to analyze in detail the logical structure and meaning of the poem. This, indeed, is but to follow the natural order of things, for the rhythm acquires its *specific* effect only in conjunction with the particular words and meaning of the poem.

In the first three stanzas, the landscape description conveys a kind of sensuous delight in the energy and fertility of uncultivated Nature. This is partly a result of the energetic verbs, partly, of the extraordinary adjectives, which possess nearly verbal force. The rhythm of these stanzas serves to reinforce the meaning and feeling of the whole, even while it attains its specific quality through its co-existence with this meaning. This rhythm does *not* imitate the brook or the countryside described in the poem; rather it expresses directly the kind of feeling I have tried to define and which is an effect of the meaning and structure of the whole poem.

We may say, then, that the specific quality of feeling in a poem is a function of its particular rhythm *and* its particular meaning. Yet it is also true that rhythm and words are distinct causative elements in the poem, even though they cannot *actually* be separated from each other. When we speak of rhythm as *actually* separate, we are not referring to rhythm but to *meter*—that ideal temporal norm, which may be associated with a *class* or *genus* of feeling, and which serves as the basis for many particular rhythms and their correlative specific feelings. Strictly speaking, the rhythm of a poem cannot be abstracted from its actual embodiment in the poem.

An illustration may ·help to clarify the point. The following
stanza is in the same meter as Hopkins' "Inversnaid"; its rhythm
is as close to Hopkins' as I could make it. The words and meaning, of course, are quite different.

> This rust-holed heap, handbrake broke,
> Her grunt-grind firebox gasping smoke,
> In rut and in road she shudders and sighs,
> Stalls and close to the curbstone dies.

The rhythmic *effect* of these (uninspired) lines is palpably different from that of Hopkins' "Inversnaid"; and it is clear that
this difference is mainly a result of the difference in the meaning
with which the rhythm co-exists. Of course the rhythm itself is
different: Altered wording and syntax, and consequent differences in syllable duration and pause pattern, makes this inevita-
ble. But the new rhythm is similar enough to the old, I think, to
make the point: The precise feeling elicited by the rhythm of a
poem depends upon the meaning with which the rhythm co-exists.

It is difficult to find a good analogue for this complex inter-
relationship. There may be an imperfect parallel in the relation
of background music to the visual content of a motion picture.
On the one hand, the background music (if it is effective) qualifies the visual effect of a sequence; on the other, the music
attains its precise effect only in close connection with the visual
or dramatic sequence. The analogy is, however, imperfect, because the music and the sequence may stand alone.

What is further suggested by the comparison is that the meter
which serves as the basis for both rhythms has a sort of generic
potentiality: In either case the rhythm produces intense and relatively simple feeling. So that we may say that this meter is of such
a genus and that this genus limits the species of rhythm which
may be produced with this meter. This meter, for example, would
be inappropriate for a complex, serious, meditative poem about
man's dependence on God. Perhaps meters may be classified in a
general way, much as Plato and Aristotle do in assigning different
kinds of *ethos* to different musical modes.

My second text for analysis, Theodore Roethke's "My Papa's

Waltz," is a somewhat more complex poem than "Inversnaid."
(As before, I will scan the first stanza.)

The whís/key ón/your breath

Could máke/a smáll/boy díz/zy

But Í/hung ón/like déath:

Such wáltz/ing wás/not eás/y.

We romped until the pans
Slid from the kitchen shelf;
My mother's countenance
Could not unfrown itself.

The hand that held my wrist
Was battered on one knuckle;
At every step you missed
My right ear scraped a buckle.

You beat time on my head
With a palm caked hard by dirt,
Then waltzed me off to bed
Still clinging to your shirt.

Here the iambic trimeter quatrain, varied with feminine endings,
trochaic and anapest substitutions, is traditional; it is traditionally associated with simple, full-feeling songs. But this is to indicate only the general potentiality of the meter. The rhythm,
though more restrained than the rhythm of "Inversnaid," has a
similar vigor and athletic gusto. It seems to convey, beside sheer
pleasure in physical motion, a kind of pure, uncomplicated delight. It attains its specific nature, however, only through its
co-existence with the meaning and words of the poem, just as
this meaning is itself qualified by its co-existence with this
rhythm.

The descriptive details about the father (the battered knuckle,
the caked palm) suggest the child's love for the father and, perhaps, the father's male roughness. There is also a touch of fear
resulting from the father's whiskey-stimulated wildness, a fear
which enhances the boy's enjoyment of the dance. The mother's
disapproval serves to indicate both the dangerousness of the
dance and the mother's separateness—her incomprehension of

the male world which father and son share during the dance.
None of these details would have these precise connotations, however, if they did not co-exist with the poem's rhythm. The rhythm
transmutes papa's waltz into a rough and unpremeditated ritual
celebrating the child's and the father's mutual love. On the side
of meaning, the most powerful touch is the last line, which
focuses the whole poem: the boy clings to his father's shirt
because, being weak and dependent, he *must* cling to avoid falling, and because he loves his father. The clinging thus epitomizes
the elemental bond between father and son and the speaker's
awareness of this bond.

The rhythm of the poem *does* imitate the waltz described in
the poem; this is possible because a waltz is a rhythmic phenomenon. The *essential* function of the poem's rhythm, however,
is to express the kind of feeling I have tried to define. And the
precise nature of this rhythm and its specific effect are not determined merely by its meter but by its co-existence with the particular words and meanings of the poem.

This analysis makes it clear that we *cannot* say much about
rhythm itself and its relation to meaning. The two poems I have
analyzed are relatively "easy" ones; yet I have been able only to
indicate their meters and to impute to their rhythms a general
class of feeling. If this seems a discouragingly negative conclusion, I might point out that it is surely better to say nothing
about rhythmic effects than to deceive oneself and others with
statements based on fallacious theories.

In the light, moreover, of what we have discovered of the
dependence of specific rhythms and specific rhythmic effects upon
their particular verbal embodiments, our conclusion would appear
to be not entirely negative, after all. For this means that we can
indirectly describe the kind of feeling elicited by particular
rhythms by analyzing the verbal structure of the poems in which
they inhere, and from which—at least partially—their precise
effects derive. This is, in fact, what I have done—what I have in
a way been forced to do—in my struggle to describe the rhythmic
effects of "Inversnaid" and "My Papa's Waltz." In order to describe
accurately the effects of these poems—in order to interpret them

—I have had to analyze their verbal, logical and dramatic structures. And this is what good critics of poetry have always done.

It is not only in the criticism of poetry that we face this problem; it faces us in all the arts. For a large element in the effect of any art is *feeling*. And yet when it comes to defining this feeling—like all human feeling, infinitely rich and various—we have a hopelessly inadequate vocabulary. Hope, fear, joy, anger, sadness, love—we have perhaps a dozen names for feeling. But they are all mere class names which cannot define the particular shade of feeling (or the complex of feelings) which we find in a poem. What we must do in this situation is abandon the attempt to define feeling directly and concentrate, instead, on analyzing and describing its cause, its object.

I take it that all human feeling is a function of (1) the personality and history of the subject and (2) the occasion, situation, experience or thought which the mind grasps and to which the organism responds. Human feeling, in other words, whether simple or complex, is commensurate with its object, as qualified by the particular subject's individual nature. (I assume a normative *human* nature common to all men whatever their personal differences, and so a norm of human feeling, too. Unless there is such a norm, I do not see how we can understand any feeling except our own.) The feeling occasioned by a poem, as contrasted with "real" objects, is also dependent upon both object and subject, but the poetic object can elicit more precise feeling than real objects. It is also more available to rational analysis than real objects, which are immersed in the flux and complexity of the world. If we are to describe the feeling elicited by a poem, then, we may do so by analyzing and describing precisely the linguistic, ideational and symbolic structure of the poem. Our description will be precise in proportion to the accuracy with which we can describe this structure, the feeling's object.

We can thus indirectly describe the rhythmic effect of a poem, even though we cannot describe rhythm itself. And because we cannot describe rhythm itself, we must understand prosodic theory and how rhythm is produced. We must learn to *produce* the rhythm of a poem, to read well, so that we may make that rhythm *present* to ear and mind. Only by performing it well can we indicate to others and to ourselves the precise rhythm of a poem. We may be only saying "listen." But if we are performing well and our listeners are really listening, that is a great deal to do.

NOTES FOR CHAPTER FIVE

1. I shall use the word "meaning" to refer to the thought and feeling attributable to the words of the poem and to the poem itself apart from their rhythm.

2. *Understanding Poetry,* pp. 118–119.

3. It ought to be apparent that the rhythm of a poem is not a sign or a pattern of signs, though it depends for its existence on signs. It is just because words are *instrumental* signs, i.e., because they exist *as* sounds apart from their sign-function, and because language is linear, that language can serve as a "carrier" of meter and rhythm.

4. See *Politics* VIII.v.1340a (trans. B. Jowett), where Aristotle remarks that visible objects have slight resemblance to moral qualities, because "figures and colours are not imitations, but signs, of moral habits, indications which the body gives of states of feeling. . . . On the other hand, even in mere melodies there is an imitation of character. . . . The same principles apply to rhythms. . . ." Aristotle's "signs" here would seem to correspond to "natural signs" in our terms.

Else points out (p. 28) that Aristotle in this passage is speaking, not of "imitations" (as the passage is usually translated), but of "likenesses"—*homoiomata.* Else comments: "Actually the relation is one of analogy: the motions of the soul have a kinship with those of music . . . so that it is moved in a manner *corresponding* to the original states of which the song is an 'imitation.' " As will be seen, this view supports my own.

5. A passage in the *Problems* (XIX.27) suggests this correspondence between rhythm and the soul's activity: "Is it because that which is heard alone has movement? . . . This movement resembles moral character both in the rhythms and in the melodic disposition of the high and low notes . . . This does not occur in other objects or sense-perception. Now these movements are connected with action, and actions are indicative of moral character." (Trans. E. S. Forster)

Susanne K. Langer, in *Feeling and Form* (New York, 1953), p. 32, comes close to the view I am arguing for in her discussion of music: ". . . music is 'significant form,' and its significance is that of a symbol, a highly articulated sensuous object, which by virtue of its dynamic structure can express the forms of vital experience which language is peculiarly unfit to convey." I would, of course, disagree with Mrs. Langer about language. As I have tried to show, when language is used to make poems, it becomes eminently fit to convey the "forms of vital experience."

6. For an excellent description of proper verse reading, see Yvor Winters, "The Audible Reading of Poetry," in *The Function of Criticism* (Denver, 1957), pp. 81–100.

7. *Practical Criticism* (New York: Harvest Books, 1929), p. 341.

CHAPTER SIX

THE NATURE OF LITERARY GENRES

THE THEORY OF literary genres, Northrop Frye has observed, "is stuck precisely where Aristotle left it."[1] One reason for this, I think, is that critics have tended to steer clear of the topic; they seem to have reached a gentlemen's agreement not to raise a vexatious and irresolvable issue. The subject fairly bristles with difficulties; it leads us to the borders of epistemology and metaphysics. Yet it is surely too important to be ignored. For the problem of genre confronts us every time we set out to interpret or evaluate a literary work. Is *Troilus and Cressida* a tragedy or a comical satire? Criticism cannot avoid the question, though critics may suppress it. On its answer (explicit or implicit) depend our interpretation and our evaluation of the play.

In their *Theory of Literature,* Wellek and Warren maintain that the literary kind

> is not a mere name, for the aesthetic convention in which the work participates shapes its character. . . . the literary kind is an "institution." It exists, not as an animal exists or even as a building . . . but as an institution exists. One can work through, express himself through, existing institutions, create new ones, or get on, so far as possible, without sharing in politics or rituals; one can also join, but then reshape, institutions.[2]

Wellek and Warren do not tell us, however, how a work "participates" in a convention, or how a genre comes into being, or what exactly its function is. I should like to attempt answers to these questions, starting from the assumption that literary genres are real in some sense. Their reality is certified, I should say, when even those critics who take a nominalist stance are compelled to *use* genre-concepts in order to speak intelligibly about the history of literature or about particular works.[3]

I

Let me begin by distinguishing the genres from the "modes" with which they are sometimes confounded. The modes, first defined by Plato, are the classifications of literature based on the form of address or the degree of "impersonation." A speaker may speak in his own person (as in third person narrative), or through fictive persons (as in drama or in first person narrative), or in a mixture of both methods (as in epic or in most novels). One may assign the lyric poem to the first or second category, depending on whether one conceives of the speaker of the lyric as the author or as a persona. These modes, rooted in the nature of language, can be used to classify all imaginative literature. The resultant classification, however, has only minimal utility for the literary critic.

Aristotle has two additional differentia of poetic imitation: the means (speech, melody, rhythm) and the object, the kind of human action imitated. Along with mode, these differentia provide a scheme whereby any literary work may be classified. It enables us to establish valid literary genres on formal grounds: in terms, that is, of object, manner (or mode), and means. It is in terms of this scheme that Aristotle defines tragedy. The genres thus established do provide a framework for discourse about particular works; but the framework is still too general to throw much light on the particular works subsumed by it. What is needed, it seems, is a method of establishing more specific genres —if that is not a contradiction in terms. A possible key to such a method may lie in Aristotle's definition of tragedy. He defines tragedy not only in terms of its object, manner and means, but in terms also of its distinctive effect: the arousal and purgation of pity and fear. This does not, as is often assumed, involve Aristotle in a kind of impressionism. The effect of tragedy is a *function* of its form; it is discerned by way of an analysis of that form. The effect—the *dynamis*—of the genre is the distinctive general effect elicited by the distinctive general form of tragedy.

There is nothing *a priori* about this formulation. It proceeds from the "facts" of actual literary works. A certain group of works has certain common structural features: such-and-such a plot, such-and-such characters, such-and-such diction, etc. This group also has in common a distinctive general effect, attributable to the general form of the group. We may say, then, that this group belongs to one genre, defined in terms of the group's general form and effect. The concept of genre thus arrived at is no' an *a priori* concept; it is not deduced from certain higher or more general principles. It is a *norm* inferred from specific actual works. And this method might be used to establish as many genres as appear to exist or to be distinguishable in the whole body of individual literary works known to us.

Such a scheme of genres would appear to provide the basis for a critical method. Yet when we come to close quarters with a particular work, if we are faithful to its individuality, our genre-concept, thus derived, again appears to be inadequate. Even when applied to Greek tragedies, the Aristotelian definition provides only a general framework for analysis. The uniqueness and complexity of each play show up sharply against the simplicity and generality of the genre-concept. *Yet this is itself a means of illuminating the specific work: of seeing its individuality more clearly than we could in the absence of a genre-concept.* General though the genre-concept must be (that is, in relation to the particular work), the more carefully inferred and the more accurately formulated it is, the more clearly it will help us to see. (I suppose that we are now in the realm of epistemology; we are glancing at the question of the necessity of general ideas for human knowledge as such.)

The genre-concept, then, *is* of considerable utility to the critic in his attempt to understand particular plays. Tragedy, as defined by Aristotle, does help us to understand Shakespeare's tragedies, since, at a certain level of generality, there are real similarities between Shakespearean and Sophoclean tragedy. Furthermore, the Aristotelian genre-concept enables us to discern the *differences* between the two forms and so to elaborate the formal features peculiar to each form. We may thus bring our genre-concept closer—make it more nearly specific—to the particular play, be it *Oedipus Rex* or *Othello*. The genre-concept enables us to classify a work, to understand the general relation between its form and effect, and even to comprehend more fully its individuality. Yet the genre-concept can never adequately describe any particular play or poem. It can never provide the perception and insight 'of a trained literary intelligence. It can, however, provide one of the conditions necessary for that intelligence to operate efficiently and accurately.

II

How do literary genres come into being? How do they inhere in, or inform, particular works? And what is their mode of being? Every literary work, whatever its similarities to other works, is *sui generis*. It seems impossible, however, to speak intelligibly about literature without using genre-concepts. That is our dilemma.

Let us assume for the moment that the traditional genres are purely nominal, arbitrary class-names assigned for "convenience" to certain groups of literary works. These class-names will then have no real reference; the distinctions on which they are based will be neither inherent in the literary works described nor derived from a rational principle. Such a version of genres might plausibly be inferred from the *Poetics*. Aristotle, we might suppose, is looking over all the literature known to him. He is most interested in the drama, and he sees that the drama is distinguishable into two main kinds (comedy and tragedy) in terms of their different objects or kinds of action, being similar in manner and means. He then goes on to elaborate this difference as regards tragedy, in terms of plot, character, diction, effect. Comedy and tragedy are clearly not natural species, like biological ones. Being made by men, they are subject to the indeterminacy of the human mind. They cannot have the same ontological status as species which are not subject to the human will.[4]

But even assuming this indeterminacy, once these kinds of drama have been created, *they inevitably become "models" for succeeding playwrights*. (This is true, I think, whether a literary theorist defines these kinds or not.) In cultures descended from, or incorporating aspects of, Greek culture (like our own), the existence of these models make it virtually impossible for new

plays to be created which are not to some extent influenced by
the forms of these works or by the idea of form to be derived
from them. In this way, comedy and tragedy have become, for
playwright and audience, *conventional forms.* Knowing the comic
and tragic plays which are part of their culture, playwright and
audience approach the making or hearing of any new play in the
light of this knowledge. As with any convention, this knowledge
constitutes an implicit compact between playwright and audience.
The expectations of the audience will depend, not only on the
structure of the play being seen, but to some extent on the intersubjective idea of its *genre.*

I have presented a *logical* explanation of the coming-to-be of
genres. It would be fatuous to believe that the process I have
described is an historical account—which we can probably never
know and do not need to know. But if the logical explanation is
valid, it means that genres are rooted in history; that they are
derived from the creation in time of actual literary works; and
that they have the same ontological status as other literary conventions.[5] Like other literary conventions, genres exist, not as
physical things, but as ideas in human minds within cultural
groups.[6] Genres are a part of culture and have themselves a
history. Sophocles' notion of tragedy is different from Shakespeare's. Yet Shakespearean tragedy is related, however distantly, to Sophoclean tragedy; and *Death of a Salesman* is related,
however distantly, to both.

To understand the works of the past, we need to recover the
conventions of the past. And we need to recover these conventions also to understand the works of the present. For these conventions have a history of their own, and we cannot understand
their present form unless we see what lies behind them. It is precisely because conventions have a history that we may properly
use the names "comedy" and "tragedy" for the plays of our time.

III

How, exactly, does a genre-concept "determine" the form of
a particular work? Or, to put it differently, how can a work
"belong" to a certain genre and yet be unique?

Anyone who has attempted to write a play or a poem has probably found himself seeking, perhaps unconsciously, for a model, for some shape or pattern to guide his own hand amidst the virtual infinitude of possibilities open to him. Or perhaps the form of his own work simply "comes to him." In either case, the form he finally creates will resemble certain other works, with which he may or may not be familiar. So long as he is part of a culture, the writer cannot avoid conceiving of his work in the light of already existing works. He may or may not "imitate" a particular play or lyric poem. But he cannot escape from some kind of formal dependence on the works of the past—any more than he can communicate without the language system he inherits. Genres represent for him (whether he believes in their existence or not) the kinds of potential form for literary expression.

Knowledge of the genres, whether abstract or habitual, assists the writer in his struggle to create something *new*. A *general* form is provided him, which enables him to get on with the shaping of particulars, to make the new work which expresses his own vision and voice.[7] Even the writer who deliberately rejects tradition unwittingly pays tribute to it, for it is precisely *that* against which he rebels and which determines the direction of his departures from it.

How then is the genre-concept related to the particular work which this concept, in some degree, formally causes? This relation may be illuminated, I believe, by considering the relation between meter and its individual embodiment in particular poems. A meter (in English verse, at any rate) is an ideal temporal norm, as I have tried to show in preceding chapters. It is never actualized in a poem, though it is inferred from the words of the poem as they are uttered in time. It is a conventional norm, existing intersubjectively in the minds of poet and hearer. A rhythm, on the other hand, is actualized in the audible reading of a poem. It arises out of the felt tension between the spoken stress pattern and the ideal metrical norm.

Now a genre is also inferred from actual works; it is also an ideal or intersubjective norm. The actual work, furthermore, is

analogous to an actual rhythm in its relation to its genre in that
it simultaneously "contains" the genre and actualizes departures
from it. Every particular work is thus unique in that it departs
from its generic norm to some degree. Sometimes the departure
may be emphatic. The peculiar charm, for example, of Shakespeare's "When icicles hang by the wall" resides, in part, in its
use of barnyard diction and imagery in a conventionally pastoral
form. More obvious instances occur in mock epic and in most
parody.

A rhythm is always particular and concrete, and it directly
imitates human feeling. A meter is a norm that serves both to
produce rhythm and to delimit the kinds of rhythm (and the
kinds of feeling) which are possible in poems making use of it.
A particular poem's rhythm is determined partly by the poem's
words and their disposition, partly by the poem's meter. Different meters possess different rhythmic possibilities; or, to put it
differently, each meter limits the kinds of rhythm and, consequently, the kinds of feeling, which are possible in poems making
use of that meter.

The genres, I think, function in a similar way. For the genres
are also intersubjective norms, and they are also, to some degree,
formative in the production of particular works. The genres serve
as ideal forms (or norms) of feeling, from which innumerable
particular and actual forms may take their shape, even while
these particular forms differ from the norms to which they
"belong."

Aristotle defines tragedy in terms of its *general* formal elements
and its *general* effect. His definition describes no particular tragedy; it describes tragedy-in-general, tragedy as a generic form
or a norm. The arousal of pity and fear does not adequately
describe the complex effect of *Othello* or the effect of any particular play. But these terms *do* delimit the *class* of feeling
within which the effect of any particular tragedy may be uniquely
defined. Similarly, the general *formal* requirements of tragedy,
as laid down in the *Poetics,* establish the formal norms within
which any particular tragedy attains its own form.

Tragedy, then, and other such generic forms, have the status
of literary conventions: They are ideal norms which serve to

establish the expectations of writer and audience. They are, in a way, expressive devices, since they aid both writer and audience to either create or comprehend works of literature. They are *not* mechanical patterns into which writers pour the "content" of their art. Nor are they definable in terms of the rigid "rules" of the neo-classical critic. Their definition must be general enough to allow for a multitude of "variations"—to allow, indeed, for possibilities which cannot be anticipated (Shakespearean tragedy and comedy, for example). And, at the same time, their definition must be specific enough to be relevant and useful. Before such "new" forms as Shakespearean tragedy and comedy could be born, there had to occur significant changes in the culture and sensibility of Western man. Yet Shakespeare's tragedies *are* tragedies, and they would not be what they are if Sophocles and Euripides and Seneca had not written before Shakespeare.

Neither comedy nor tragedy are actual forms; they exist only as intersubjective norms. Particular comedies and tragedies do exist; they relate to comedy and tragedy (the genres) as individuals relate to universals. The genres may be defined in terms of their general form and their correlative general effect; but the form and effect of any particular work can be truly specified only in terms of its particular plot, character, thought, diction, etc., the form which it alone possesses and which expresses its own action and meaning. Yet such a specification is facilitated and, indeed, made precise, by the knowledge of the genre to which the particular work belongs. This is why it is proper to say that a particular tragedy belongs to that genre and yet say that it is a unique work. It has the general form of plays which arouse pity and fear; and it is so individuated that it is unlike any other actual play.

IV

I have said that the genres, like rhythms, *directly* imitate human action. To clarify this idea, I need to distinguish between representative and rhythmic imitation. Representative imitation (in literature) involves the use of language to make or "create" the natural signs of human action—to make the fictive speech and the human acts which imitate character, thought, feeling.

These images, patterned into a play or novel or lyric poem, themselves imitate the human action which is the ultimate object of imitation, Rhythmic imitation, on the other hand, bypasses the intermediate stages of this process: It makes no use of natural signs or of images. Rather, as in the case of verse rhythm, it *directly* imitates human action or feeling; it can do this because, being a temporal pattern, it corresponds in its movement to the "movement" of the soul.

A play or novel or lyric poem, since its medium is language, is essentially a linear or temporal art—it actualizes itself in time. Thus the shape of a literary work is a temporal shape: a pattern of feeling, of aroused expectations which are either disappointed or fulfilled, or both at once, *in time*. This temporal pattern is a rhythm, a diffuse one compared to verse rhythm, but a rhythm nonetheless. It attains its effect, as does verse rhythm, by directly imitating human feeling. This rhythm is what Kenneth Burke refers to as "the curve of feeling" in a work of literature, the structuring of the audience's psychology.[8] And this rhythm is related to genre as verse rhythm relates to meter.

Let me emphasize that I am not referring to the spectator's general response to, say, *Macbeth*—his pity or fear or hope or anger, either from moment to moment or as a consummation at the end of the play. This sort of effect involves representative imitation. We are now *not* speaking of particular responses as such, but of the *patterning of responses in time,* their arrangement in such a way as to make a rhythm which itself directly imitates human feeling. It is apparent that this rhythmic pattern is, in a sense, parasitic: It depends for both its existence and its shape on the representative, much as verse rhythm depends on the particular words and their disposition in a poem for its precise nature. This means that representation in literature (as contrasted with music) has an importance at least equal to rhythmic imitation. *The rhythmic cannot exist in literature without the representative.*[9] And this, of course, calls into question all theories of "pure poetry," any attempt to reduce literature to the status of music.

We might surmise, from these speculations, that the genres do embody *general patterns or norms of human feeling* which, when they are particularized and actualized in specific works, "become" the rhythmic patterns which directly imitate human feeling. But is there anything *natural* about these norms? That is to say: Are the *forms* of the genres *necessary* or merely a matter of chance? The genres arose, we have argued, in history. Since they were created by men, their forms were subject to the imperfection and indeterminacy attendant upon any human product. Their forms, it would seem to follow, should be contingent, not necessary. On the other hand, if we assume a *human* nature, their forms cannot be wholly indeterminate. They are produced by men for men who possess that nature.

If we grant that the genres are conventional norms of human feeling, then we may say that the genres are natural as any product of human nature is natural. So far, that is, as human nature is part of nature, there are determinate kinds of human feeling. It follows that literary works produced by and for human beings, works which embody human feeling, must be determined or limited by human nature. The *classes* of human feeling are obviously not unlimited, though particular individuations of feeling may be. The genres are ideal patterns or classes of human feeling; when these ideal and general patterns are actualized and particularized in specific works, they become patterns of particular feeling within the generic class.

This is not to say that the currently-known genres are exhaustive, that new genres may not be born. It is to say that the genres we now have (so far as we have accurately defined them) are "natural" in the sense indicated, and that genres are limited in kind and number by the possibilities of human feeling. Within each class of feeling, the possible individuations are perhaps infinite: They can be as various as the variations in artists, in languages, in cultures. But the individual artist is limited by his humanity to those classes of human feeling of which human beings are capable.[10]

V

The archetypal school of criticism, whose theoretical bases have most recently been expounded by Northrop Frye, is, so far as I can judge, mainly engaged in discerning in all literature just those general norms which we have called genres.[11] It is true that Frye distinguishes between genres and myths; but his "myths" are only genres "essentialized"; that is, instead of being defined in terms of their general structure and effect, they are defined as generalized stories. One can hardly quarrel with this. I have been urging the utility for the critic of such norms. What is disturbing is that, in the usual practice of archetypal critics, the chief aim seems to be the discovery of such myths as an end in itself—as if that constituted the whole purpose of literary criticism. Such a procedure is patently reductive: It reduces all works to a few common patterns. The aim, as Frank Kermode remarks, is to stand far enough back from literature to see a work "as frozen in space, devoid, like myth, of temporality, and fit for inclusion in an all-embracing mythical system."[12] The uniqueness of the work—what gives the work both its individuality and its value— would seem to be of little interest to the critic of this school.

The critic who assumes the existence of genres also is concerned with common forms in literature. But, for him, the discovery of these forms is not an end in itself. It is, rather, one means of *illuminating particular works in all their individuality*. The archetypal critic tends to ignore the individuality of literary works. He believes, says Kermode, "only in criticism which has backed so far away from literature that all the little things that make one work different from another drop out of view."[13] So far as he does this, the archetypal critic is not engaging in literary criticism, but in a kind of anthropological speculation or some related and, no doubt, worthwhile study, for which literature provides him with data.

What lies behind such criticism, of course, is the assumption of a "collective unconscious," the universal presence in men and therefore in all literature of certain recurrent myths or psychic "projections." It is the presence of these which accounts for the perennial power of certain works of literature and which justifies the criticism which uncovers them. I do not have the competence to dispute the existence of a "collective unconscious." But even assuming its existence, it is nevertheless absurd to believe that its mere presence in a work can account for the work's poetic power. If this were true, then we should be able to codify the major archetypes and be content to contemplate them forever—leaving literature to the uninitiate. There seem to be real differences, furthermore, among archetype theorists, as to the precise status of the archetypes. According to some theorists, the archetypes are only projections of instinct—in which case they would be historically conditioned.[14]

One source of support for the archetypal school has been the work of the Cambridge classical anthropologists (Cornford, Frazer, Murray), who have attempted to trace Greek drama back to its roots in ancient religious ritual. It may be true that Greek (and English) drama originated in religious ritual—though how this origin was transformed into drama remains unexplained. A knowledge of this may help a critic to understand the form of the drama he seeks to interpret. But he should not confuse the *origin* of drama with its *nature*. Drama and ritual are quite different things. A person participating in a ritual (actually or vicariously) is first of all *a believer* in its reality and efficacy. He is *not* a spectator, partially identified with priest or dancer, and so engaged in a *fictive* action, partially detached and observing. The participant in ritual himself *enacts* the rite. The Catholic Mass, as I understand it, is not a drama—though it is, no doubt, highly dramatic. The believer engages in the ritual and *real* re-enactment of the Passion and Resurrection of Christ; he *really* partakes of the Body and Blood of Christ in Communion. He does not merely contemplate these as fictive or historical events: *He acts them.* The effect of such real participation is obviously quite different from the effect of a dramatic performance. The spectator is always aware that the drama is a fiction, an imitation merely.

Ritual patterns may, of course, inform certain works—as, for example, in *Oedipus Rex.* And such patterns may be deliberately insinuated in their work by authors under the spell of archetypal criticism. Faulkner's *Light in August* and Hemingway's *The Old Man and the Sea* are obvious instances of this. When such patterns (whatever their cause) are structural features of the work

—felt presences—then they are the proper concerns of the critic, for they affect the meaning of the work and the response of the spectator. Thus it is important to recognize the ambiguous status of the tragic hero as both scapegoat and saviour wherever he truly has such a status (e.g., in *Oedipus* and in *Hamlet*). But the attempt to uncover hidden archetypes or mythic patterns in all literature is, from the point of view of literary criticism, a meaningless game.[15]

VI

In a famous and much-disputed passage (*Poetics* 4.1448b), Aristotle speaks of two basic "causes" or genetic principles of poetry. According to one interpretation of the passage, these two causes are *mimesis* and *harmonia*—in the terms we have been using, representative imitation and rhythmic imitation. I would regard these as the constitutive principles of all the "representative" arts, i.e., of literature, sculpture, painting, opera, cinema. These arts, I would hold, dispense with one or the other principle at the risk of their own well-being—at the risk, indeed, of their own being. That is to say: When literature becomes "pure" sound, when it is reduced to the status of "music," it ceases to be anything *but* sound. When painting becomes perfectly non-representative, it becomes decoration. In either case, as I think has been shown with respect to literature, the rhythmic depends on the representative. On the other hand, it is also evident that exclusive dependence on representation makes for an impoverished art.

Verse rhythm and generic forms, I have argued, are instances of rhythmic imitation. The traditional genres, tragedy and comedy, are, on this view, complex norms of human feeling; they embody or articulate patterns of feeling which correspond to such patterns in the human soul. The power and longevity of these genres (within our culture) may properly be attributed to this fact.[16] The power of generic form is difficult to demonstrate, because it is virtually impossible to separate it from the representation in which it inheres. The best illustration I know is *Romeo and Juliet,* where the play's representative faults enable us to discern, by a kind of negative judgment, the rhythmic sources of the play's effectiveness.

Not that all the apparent incongruities of the play are to be censured; on the contrary, many of these have an astonishing rightness and effectiveness. The pervasive and emphatic bawdy, for example, might at first glance appear to conflict with the idealized love which stands in persistent opposition to it. In the very first scene, the oafish Samson proclaims that he will thrust the Montague's maids to the wall, that he will cut off their maidenheads, that they shall feel him while he is able to stand, etc. This is just the first instance of the rakish phallicism that pervades the play. After the first meeting of the lovers, while Romeo hides from his companions, Mercutio invokes his friend:

> I conjure thee by Rosaline's bright eyes,
> By her high forehead and her scarlet lip,
> By her fine foot, straight leg, and quivering thigh,
> And the demesnes that there adjacent lie. . . .
> (II.i.17–20)

When Benvolio remarks that this will anger Romeo, Mercutio replies:

> This cannot anger him. 'Twould anger him
> To raise a spirit in his mistress' circle
> Of some strange nature, letting it there stand
> Till she had laid it and conjured it down.
> (II.i.23–26)

And he concludes: "Oh, that she were/An open etcetera, thou a poperin pear!" This sort of thing, this gross, nearly childish phallicism, occurs not only in comic scenes, but is an undercurrent in passages where the purest love is being expressed. "I must be gone and live, or stay and die," says Romeo on his post-nuptial morning.

Now this bawdiness actually intensifies, rather than interferes with, the central feeling of the play. It directly evokes in the spectator the wild eroticism which underlies the youthful and idealized passion of the lovers. It calls up, in short, the sexual impulse which is the efficient cause of, and is transmuted into, the paradoxically pure love of the adolescent. At the same time, the realist-bawdy vision of love establishes more firmly the world of workaday reality against which the lovers are pitted and by which they are destroyed. The play's violent shifts in mood, moreover, contribute to the play's over-all atmosphere of violence and irrationality.

The play's unity *is* seriously impaired by contradictory and shifting views of the general cause of the lovers' misfortune. In the Prologue two different causes are suggested:

> From forth the fatal loins of these two foes
> A pair of star-cross'd lovers take their life;
> Whose misadventur'd piteous overthrows
> Doth with their death bury their parents' strife.

The lovers must die in order to assuage their parents' hatred; but they must also die because there is a kind of inscrutable fatality in their passion. The former view is emphasized at the end of the play, in the Prince's "See what a scourge is laid upon your hate. . . ." and to some extent by the plot. On the other hand, the idea of their being "star-cross'd" is emphasized by the lovers themselves, by their intimations of doom (*Romeo:* ". . . my mind misgives/Some consequence, yet hanging in the stars,/Shall bitterly begin his fearful date/With this night's revels . . ." *Juliet:* "O God, I have an ill-divining soul! Methinks I see thee, now thou art below,/As one dead in the bottom of a tomb.") And the continual play of love-and-death imagery further supports this view.

In addition we get the "moral" view of things from Friar Laurence. "These violent delights have violent ends," he tells Romeo, "And in their triumph die, like fire and powder,/Which, as they kiss, consume. . . . Therefore love moderately. . . ." (II.vi.9–14) A little before this (II.iii.1–30), the Friar pronounces his philosophy about the right use and abuse of nature—which clearly applies to the lovers:

> For naught so vile that on the earth doth live
> But to the earth some special good doth give;
> Nor aught so good but, strain'd from that fair use,
> Revolts from true birth, stumbling on abuse.

The lovers, on this view, have only themselves to blame. Whether or not these views are logically contradictory, they are aesthetically disruptive, diffusing the representative form and impairing the play.

Furthermore: the play's mood is shattered again and again by sudden descents into farce. Two examples should suffice. In Act III, scene iii, the Friar lectures the desperate Romeo at great length (some fifty lines). It is, to all appearances, a serious, philosophical speech; yet its seriousness, and the authority of the Friar, are suddenly undercut by the Nurse's

> O Lord, I could have stay'd here all the night
> To hear good counsel. O, what learning is!
> (III.iii.159–60)

There is, finally, an unmistakable farcicality in the lamentation over Juliet's supposed death (IV.iv). I quote a few representative passages:

> *Nurse.* O woe! O woful, woful, woful day!
> Most lamentable day, most woful day
> That ever ever I did yet behold!
> O day! O day! O day! O hateful day! . . .
> *Paris.* Beguil'd divorced, wronged, spited, slain!
> Most detestable Death, by thee beguil'd,
> By cruel cruel thee quite overthrown!
> O love! O life! not life, but love in death!

There is a good deal more of this. That it is not a mere lapse of taste is certified by the parody of Kyd's famous lines ("O eyes, no eyes. . . ."). Shakespeare seems to be mocking his own work. But whatever the intention, such lapses seriously impair the play's tone, credibility, unity.

And for all this, the play yet retains a residue of real power, which derives, I submit, from the rhythm of feeling which is patterned there, from, in short, the play's generic form. This form is given a modern setting in *West Side Story,* where in spite of equally great faults—inept sociologizing and mediocre music—the power of the form survives.

The principle of rhythmic imitation is also involved in all those strikingly "right" structural features in literature which we cannot

explain in terms of representative imitation. Instances abound in
Shakespeare. When Romeo responds to news of Juliet's death, he
does so, not, as we might have expected, with rage, but with
resignation: "Well, Juliet, I will lie with thee tonight." And then
there are those brilliant and hard-to-explain scenes: the quarrel
scene in *Julius Caesar,* the willow scene in *Othello,* the knocking
at the gate in *Macbeth,* the galley scene in *Antony* and *Cleopatra.*
In the lyric, the rhythmic principle accounts for the effectiveness
of certain refrains (as in Wyatt's "In Eternum," Nashe's "In Time
of Pestilence"), of the juxtaposition of apparently incongruous
elements (as in Eliot), and of "qualitative progressions" that cannot be fully explained (as in the concluding stanza of "To His
Coy Mistress" or the whole development of "Among School
Children").

It is difficult to find instances of the rhythmic principle in the
novel, mainly because the novel has tended to scant the rhythmic
principle in its concern with verisimilitude. There is a striking
instance of rhythmic form in *Madame Bovary,* however. Charles is
watching Emma die; the priest is administering the final sacra-
ment. We know that Emma is only a sentimental believer, and,
throughout the novel, the Church, its doctrines, and its clergy
have been presented in the most contemptuous and satirical light.
Yet at this moment Flaubert describes with precise eloquence the
rite in whose efficacy neither he nor we believe. The result is a
passage of extraordinary rightness and power.

> The priest rose to take the crucifix. Reaching forward like one
> in thirst, she glued her lips to the body of the Man-God and laid
> upon it with all her failing strength the most mighty kiss of love
> she had ever given. The priest recited the *Misereatur* and the
> *Indulgentiam;* then he dipped his right thumb into the oil and
> began the unctions: first on the eyes, that had so coveted all
> earthly splendors; then on the nostrils, that had loved warm
> breezes and amorous perfumes; then on the mouth, that had
> opened for falsehood, had groaned with pride and cried out in
> lust; then on the hands, that had revelled in delicious contacts;
> lastly on the soles of the feet, that once had run so swiftly to
> the assuaging of her desires, and now would walk no more.
>   (Translated by Alan Russell)

This foolish and corrupt woman is dying like an animal. How can that death which by its physical horror so diminishes her raise her to tragic dignity? We no doubt see her partly through Charles's adoring eyes, but more than this is involved. There is a strange and paradoxical grandeur in Emma's death (which Flaubert may not have intended), a grandeur lent by Flaubert's eloquence and by the poignant ironic allusions to Christ's Passion and to Christian love. At this moment, we see Emma's tawdry lusts clearly as what they are: Yet we see them also as a shadowy analogue of divine love, figured in the anointing of the sensual organs of the body which is at once corrupt and beloved. The effectiveness of the passage cannot be explained in terms of representative imitation. Flaubert has caught in action a pattern of human feeling, a rhythm of the heart.

NOTES FOR CHAPTER SIX

1. Northrop Frye, *Anatomy of Criticism* (Princeton, 1957), p. 13.
2. Wellek and Warren, *Theory of Literature* (New York, 1949), p. 235.
3. Croce is a case in point. His rejection of genres (*Aesthetic,* trans. D. Ainslie, Noonday Edition [New York, 1963], pp. 35–38) appears to be based on the eighteenth-century idea that genres are *a priori,* eternal forms from which strict "laws" may be derived. Croce rightly sees that this involves a reification of class-terms, the "fallacy of misplaced concreteness," in Whitehead's happy phrase. But to argue thus is to beat a dead horse. It remains true that genres are different in status from arbitrary shelf arrangements.
4. Cf. R. McKeon, "Rhetoric and Poetic in Aristotle," in *Aristotle's Poetics and English Literature,* ed. E. Olson (Chicago, 1965), p. 229: "Art . . . is a concrete object and as such analyzable in terms of form and matter, but unlike natural objects its form and definition are not determinate or natural but are determined ultimately not only by the potentiality of the artistic material but by the nature of the artist and the susceptibilities of the audience."
5. See Harry Levin's brilliant essay on the role of convention in literature, "Literature as an Institution," *Accent* VI (1946), pp. 159–68; reprinted in *Criticism: the Foundations of Modern Literary Judgment,* ed. Schorer, Miles, and McKenzie, rev. ed. (New York, 1958), pp. 546–53).

6. Cf. Saussure, *Course in General Linguistics* (New York, 1959), pp. 17–20, on the status of language and the relation between *langue* and *parole*.

7. Levin, pp. 550–51, writes: "But art must also differ from life for technical reasons: limitations of form, difficulties of expression. The artist, powerless to overcome these obstacles by himself, must have the assistance of his audience. They must agree to take certain formalities and assumptions for granted, to take the word for the deed, the 'shading for the shadow."

8. Kenneth Burke, *Counter-statement* (Los Altos, 1953), pp. 29–44.

9. The view of art I am setting forth comes close to Susanne Langer's theory of art as a symbolic form of feeling. One difference between us ought to be noted. Since Mrs. Langer tends to think of all the arts as analogous with music, she slights the representative side of art. As I think has been shown, the efficacy of the rhythmic principle depends on the representative, through and by which it is articulated. In the absence of representation, the "representative" arts are bereft of that which actuates them as determinate forms and which grounds their power and meaning. See Langer, *Philosophy in a New Key* (Cambridge, Mass., 1960), pp. 204–19.

10. Aristotle (*Poetics* 4.1448b) attributes the differentiation of literary forms to differences in human nature: "Poetry now diverged in two directions, according to the individual character of the writers."

11. See Frye, pp. 131 ff.

12. Frank Kermode, Review of Frye's *A Natural Perspective, New York Review of Books* IV (April 22, 1965), p. 10.

13. Kermode, p. 11. I ought to remark that I do *not* include in the archetypal school such critics as C. L. Barber and W. R. B. Lewis who bring to their analysis of literature the myths or ritual patterns which inhere in the culture from which the literature emerged. This is a proper use of historically relevant knowledge; it is a quite different sort of procedure from searching for universal archetypes which presumably reside in the collective unconscious and constitute the essential meaning of any work.

14. The clearest statement of the underlying assumptions of archetypal criticism may be found in C. G. Jung's two papers, "Archetypes of the Collective Unconscious" and "The Concept of the Collective Unconscious" in *The Collected Works,* ed. Read, Fordham and Adler (New York, 1959), vol. IX, part 1, pp. 3–53.

Jung himself sees a close connection between the archetypes of the collective unconscious and the instincts; he writes (pp. 43–44):

> Medical psychology, growing as it did out of professional practice, insists on the personal nature of the psyche. . . . It is a

psychology of the person, and its aetiological or causal factors are regarded almost wholly as personal in nature. Nonetheless, even this psychology is based on certain general biological factors, for instance on the sexual instinct or on the urge for self-assertion, which are by no means merely personal peculiarities . . . the instincts are not vague and indefinite by nature, but are specifically formed motive forces which, long before there is any consciousness, and in spite of any degree of consciousness later on, pursue their inherent goals. Consequently they form very close analogies to the archetypes, so close, in fact, that there is good reason for supposing that the archetypes are the unconscious images of the instincts themselves, in other words, that they are *patterns of instinctual behavior.* [Jung's italics.]

Cf. Maud Bodkin, *Archetypal Patterns in Poetry* (Oxford, 1934), pp. 3–5.

Rollo May ("The Significance of Symbols," in *Symbolism in Religion and Literature* [New York, 1961], pp. 11–49), points out that the images that appear in the dreams of psychotherapy patients cannot be given arbitrary meaning by the therapist. Such images have meaning only for the particular dreamer, and this meaning can be discovered only by grasping its function in the dreamer's personality and life-situation. The dream symbol, May says (p. 18), "is given its power and character as a symbol by the total situation of the patient's life at that moment. This patient might dream of a cave in another dream in which it would not be a symbol, or it might have any one of an infinite number of other meanings depending upon his existence at that time. This point is important to emphasize because of some tendency in psychoanalysis to equate given words and symbols with specific meanings. This is a literalistic, fundamentalistic approach, and in my judgment it is inaccurate." Furthermore (pp. 19–20), our ability to understand particular dream symbols "depends . . . upon our capacity to participate in [the dreamer's] world and to experience the symbol from the point of view of the questions his existence poses for him."

Analogously, if the literary symbol is not a projection of the collective unconscious, its meaning cannot be arbitrary, but must be determined by understanding its function in the *literary* structure of the work in which it appears.

15. The same arguments apply to psychoanalytic criticism. The Oedipus complex may affect the behavior of Hamlet, and may help to account for both the "intractability" of the play and its perennial appeal. But it does not explain either Hamlet the Dane or *Hamlet* the play.

Jung himself has made one of the best arguments against the reductive method. In "On the Relation of Analytic Psychology to Poetic Art," *Contributions to Analytic Psychology* (London, 1929), p. 230, he writes:

> The reductive method of Freud is purely a method of medical treatment that has for its subject a morbid and unsuitable structure. This morbid structure has taken the place of normal accomplishment, and hence must be broken down before the way can be cleared for a sound adaptation. In this case the process of leading-back to a general human basis is entirely appropriate. But when applied to the work of art this method leads to the results depicted above. From beneath the shimmering robe of art it extracts the naked commonness of the elementary *homo sapiens,* to which species the poet also belongs.

16. It is reasonable to suppose that artists choose this or that genre depending on whether they perceive in it the potentiality for expressing their particular vision. The choice need not be conscious; and the artist may choose wrongly. The consequences of a bad choice would be a flawed work and its failure to survive. So it would seem that the longevity of a genre depends on the ability of the artists who use it, as well as on its intrinsic viability. Cf. Levin, p. 553.

CHAPTER SEVEN

SHAKESPEAREAN TRAGEDY

I SHOULD LIKE now to illustrate what has been abstract and speculative: the utility of genre-concepts. Specifically, I want to show how our concept of tragedy, derived from works that ante-date Shakespeare, enables us to see clearly Shakespeare's modification of the earlier forms and the distinctive shape of Shakespeare's form.

I

For Aristotle, and for most critics since Aristotle, "character" means the moral disposition of the agent of an action.[1] This is a common-sense view, substantiated by much of our real-life experience. We usually estimate the character of real people in moral terms, though we may not use the language of moral philosophy to do so. When we say that so-and-so "has character" we mean that he is morally good. It seems reasonable to suppose that we regard the fictive beings of a drama in the same way—usually, I think, we do. With Shakespeare's characters, however, we run into difficulty with this assumption. Hamlet or Othello or Lear are not adequately described by moral terms, no matter how precise or exhaustive we make them. How shall we describe Hamlet? He is dutiful, sensitive, considerate, passionate, phlegmatic, scrupulous, noble, pious, magnanimous. He is all of that; yet these traits are simply not adequate to our sense of a "reality" which does not seem measurable in moral terms at all.

I do not mean merely that Hamlet seems very real to us, that he is a "round" rather than a "flat" character. He is, of course, characterized in great detail. But one has only to recall the particularity of O'Neill's characters to realize that the distinction we

are looking for is not a quantitative one. We know (or fancy we
know) Shakespeare's great characters as we know those real
people we love. People we do not love may be just as real to us;
we may know more particulars about them. But those we love
we know in a special way: We are aware of a presence in them
which no words can describe and no facts indicate. And it is just
this mysterious quality that Shakespeare's characters possess.

I think we may approach an understanding of this special
quality as an aspect of what the Scholastics call "the person."
This is primarily a theological concept used in speculating about
the doctrine of the Trinity. The Scholastics also use it analogi-
cally to signify the pre-eminent dignity and excellence of human
beings, the only creatures in the physical order who *are* persons.
Modern Thomists explain the concept by distinguishing the person from the individual. Man is an individual, is individuated
from other human beings, by reason of the matter, the flesh and
blood, of which he is composed. All men have a common nature,
but they are not human nature as such. Because men are cor-
poreal, each man is an individual, embodying human nature in
this particular flesh and blood. But man is not just an individual,
like a dog or a rose. He is also a person.

Man does not exist, says Maritain,

> only in a physical manner. He has spiritual super-existence
> through knowledge and love; he is, in a way, a universe in him-
> self, a microcosm, in which the great universe in its entirety can
> be encompassed through knowledge; and through love he can give
> himself completely to beings who are to him as it were other
> selves, a relation for which no equivalent can be found in the.
> physical world. . . . To say that a man is a person is to say . . .
> that he is a minute fragment of matter that is at the same time a
> universe, a beggar who communicates with absolute being, mortal
> flesh whose value is eternal, a bit of straw into which heaven
> enters. It is this metaphysical mystery that religious thought
> points to when it says that the person is the image of God.[2]

That is about as far as abstract language can go in defining the
person. There is another manner of expressing it, however, one
that corresponds to our intuitive perception of selfhood, of the
infinitely receding depths of the self which the self knows can

never be fully known. In a famous passage in the *Confessions,* St. Augustine tries to discover what manner of being he is—and can find no answer. Gazing back over his life, he sees that his nature—manhood—does not adequately define himself. He sees that "there is something of man that the very spirit of man that is in him does not know." And then he goes on to descant on the vast universe of his memory, suggesting powerfully the aspect of his being which transcends his nature and puts him in touch with eternity.[3]

I submit that it is precisely this personal dimension that distinguishes the characters of Shakespeare. They are individuations of human nature and are differentiated by their specific moral traits. But they are also persons, unique selves which transcend their individual natures, worlds in themselves, capable of knowledge and love. This is why we respond to these characters and to the stories they enact as we do to those of no other dramatist. Hamlet and Macbeth are not only individuals; they are persons, too.

The idea of the person is a Christian idea. It did not exist, and probably could not have existed, before the Incarnation. For the Incarnation, the historical fact of God become man, is the very ground of the super-eminent dignity of the human person, raising man to the level of divinity while he yet remains wholly man. It should not surprise us, then, that Shakespeare possessed a sense of the person, for it was part of his culture, a culture which culminated centuries of Christian thought and feeling. The idea was absent from the culture of Sophocles, and it has almost disappeared from our own.

This is why Sophocles' characters, for all their magnificence, are never felt to be persons as Shakespeare's characters are. Oedipus and Antigone are characterized with consummate artistry— but they are individuals, not persons. We know them as it were from the "outside," as moral individuals embodying the noblest Greek ideals of human nature. But however noble this ideal, it falls short of the Christian idea of the person. For the Greek ideal, being an abstract essence, misses the existential uniqueness and the supra-humanity of the person. We cannot imagine Oedipus or Antigone outside the dramas to which they lend their names. Hamlet and Othello and Lear, as the Romantics perceived, have a kind of life of their own. This is because they are persons.

II

If Shakespeare conveys in his characters a sense of the person, we may wonder how he has managed to do so. Our own attempts to define the person have sufficiently shown its elusiveness as a concept. By what art has Shakespeare embodied the person, or, rather, an appearance of the person, in the fictive creatures of his plays? I may as well confess at once that I do not have an answer to this question. All I can do is throw out some conjectures.

I have already suggested that we are most aware of a personal dimension in those we love. And it is perhaps significant that those who attempt to elucidate the idea of the person turn at some point to a consideration of human love. Take, for example, this passage, quoted by Father D'Arcy in *The Mind and Heart of Love:*

> Nothing is more intimate to our selves than this mysterious I who is the underlying subject of our acts and the term beyond which one cannot go in the line of willing. "I" and "Me", and that is all. But what a mystery! See how this absolute and this incommunicable being cannot find peace in itself. It will seek— and it is not some *other thing* which it will seek, for things cannot interest it nor satisfy it—it will seek *another* I, which it will long to make its own in order to discover itself there and to lose itself. And this second I and this second Me is nevertheless also an absolute and incommunicable. It matters not. Irresistibly they will go the one to the other, for they live for one another. The person is absolute, yes, but it is also relative. . . . To be a person is to be essentially in search of a person. Love presupposes knowledge, but it can to some degree do without it; what it needs is the living and actual being itself. For a person there must be a person.[4]

Now if loving is, in a way, an activation, a revelation, of the person, this may be a clue to one of the ways in which Shakespeare conveys personality. It is noteworthy, at any rate, that he places some of the most impressive of his characters in relations of love to others.

We have Othello and Desdemona, Lear and Cordelia, Antony and Cleopatra. Is it not just when these characters are expressing love that we are most keenly aware of them as persons? In the last act of *King Lear,* after the old man has realized his madness in rejecting Cordelia, his mind clears for a moment. He recognizes his beloved daughter and speaks to her. The passage is extraordinary: Its plainness and quietness are highly eloquent—as if the feeling to be expressed were so profound that it can be articulated only by all that is left unsaid. We get the appearance of natural, unaffected speech; not the speech of a King, but that of a heart-broken old man:

> Be your tears wet? Yes, faith. I pray weep not.
> If you have poison for me, I will drink it.
> I know you do not love me; for your sisters
> Have, as I do remember, done me wrong.
> You have some cause, they have not. (IV.vii.71–74)

Cordelia replies: "No cause, no cause." And with those words Cordelia becomes for us a person. In terms of logic or legal justice, she *has* cause. But "causes" do not operate on the level of persons.

A little later, while they are being led to prison, Lear utters his joy in having recovered his pearl in verse that is nearly merry:

> When thou dost ask me blessing, I'll kneel down
> And ask of thee foreigiveness. So we'll live,
> And pray, and sing, and tell old tales, and laugh
> At gilded butterflies, and hear poor rogues
> Talk of court news: and we'll talk with them too—
> Who loses and who wins; who's in, who's out—
> And take upon 's the mystery of things,
> As if we were God's spies; and we'll wear out,
> In a wall'd prison, packs and sects of great ones
> That ebb and flow by th' moon. (V.iii.10–19)

That is precisely the right tone: at once joyous and self-effacing, at once solemn-sad and merry. It is the tone of one who, having discovered the absolute value of a beloved person, regards all things sublunary as trivial—as, in a way, absurd.

III

But we have not, after all, answered the question we started with. To observe that Shakespeare makes lovers of some of his characters is only to say that he selects actions potentially revealing of persons. It is clearly not to account for all those characters who are not lovers. If we are to explain how the person is actualized by Shakespeare, we will have to find grounds more relative than this. I venture another conjecture.

Those dramatic conventions which Professor Schücking calls "primitive devices" are rarely, in Shakespeare, quite as unnatural and implausible as Schücking makes them out to be. These conventions, furthermore, as Schücking himself recognizes, vary a good deal in the degree of their unnaturalness. At one extreme, for example, there is the purely expository ("primitive") aside of Desdemona, when she suddenly breaks off her banter with Iago and informs the audience that "I am not merry, but I do beguile / The thing I am by seeming otherwise" (II.i.123–24). At the other extreme, there is Hamlet's "natural," in-character: "A little more than kin and less than kind" (I.ii.65). Somewhere in between, neither direct nor indirect, neither quite nature nor quite unnatural, we get such an utterance as Iago's symbolically reverberating "I am not what I am" (I.i.65).

So, too, with the soliloquy. Sometimes we get the natural self-revelations of Hamlet; sometimes, the nearly direct speeches of Iago or Edmund. Now Shakespeare was the master, not the slave, of the conventions of his theatre, and he used them—at times transmuted them—for his particular ends. But his art is a mixed or "impure" art, at one moment conventional and un-realistic, at another verisimilar and naturalistic. How can such a mixture of methods "work" as well as it does? There can be little question that it does work, that it works indeed much better than the "pure" naturalism of an O'Neill. I think we are now in a position to say why.

First of all, through a degree of realism in the presentation of character and motive, Shakespeare represents the *particular moral nature* of his characters—just as O'Neill does. But Shakespeare goes beyond this, and it is just the "unnatural" side of his art that enables him to do so. The very impurity of his art enables him to create characters who are both individuals and persons.[5]

Take, for example, the matter of Othello's jealousy. Rymer, limited by a simpleminded theory of verisimilitude and decorum, finds Othello's jealousy inconsistent with his typical nature and therefore absurd. Professor Stoll, on the other hand, counters Rymer's rationalism with a somewhat more sophisticated irrationalism. He grants the inconsistency and absurdity, yet holds it to be a quality of the greatest dramatic art. It is just the contrast between the doer and his deed which makes for the intense emotional impact, which, for Professor Stoll, is the be-all, end-all of tragedy.[6]

Stoll perceives, in short, the absence of natural motivation, and he also perceives the *emotional coherence* which, in the theatre, quite overrides any rational scruple. But he draws from these fine perceptions the wrong conclusion. Emotional coherence does not stem from mere sensational contrast (the melodramatic thriller would then be equal to *Othello*); it stems rather from a more profound coherence than may at first appear, a coherence between character at its deepest level, and action.

Now as a matter of fact there is much in the play that "explains" Othello's jealousy on the naturalistic level. Iago's deceptive powers are carefully and emphatically developed. Desdemona is pitifully unsophisticated in the ways of the world—she is too innocent to be prudent. And Othello himself—egotistical, inexperienced, credulous, even, perhaps, a little stupid—is not too difficult a mark for Iago. Yet there remains (why not admit it?) a *sense* of inconsistency, of absurdity—a sense of something almost *formal* about Othello's falling into so terrible a passion. We are at once convinced of the reality of his jealousy and at a loss, ultimately, to explain it. And it is just this mystery, I think, which makes us aware of a fount of motive beyond psychology and of a dimension of being deeper than the individual.

I would put the matter thus. The apparent absence of cause—a gap in nature—opens up the spectator's imagination to the personal depths of character. Through the verse Othello speaks at crucial moments, we are convinced of the reality and integrity of the *person* acting—however unsure we may be of his motives. Between such moments, and given direction by them, the imagi-

nation interpolates the personal causes of action. This is why we
are aware in the theatre of a consistency which we cannot wholly
explain in rational terms. Consistency there is, and of a high
order, but it can be apprehended fully only by way of the
imagination.

"It is the cause, it is the cause, my soul." The "it" in Othello's
superb line has no referent. Neither Othello nor we can name it,
for it has no name. But it exists, and it is the cause.

IV

Shakespeare's fellow dramatists shared both his culture and
the conventions of his theatre; yet none of them created characters who are persons. In pointing to his culture and the conventions of his theatre, we have singled out conditions, not causes.
We are therefore led to suppose that Shakespeare possessed two
powers to a degree far surpassing his fellows. First of all, he must
have been able to *conceive* of persons—perhaps it would be more
accurate to say "imagine" persons. Secondly, he must have had
the mimetic power to objectify such imagined beings. This
mimetic power is, I think, inseparable in Shakespeare from his
power over language, inseparable from his greatness as a poet.

Few critics take Shakespeare's mastery of dramatic verse as
seriously as (I think) they should. For verse—the controlled
rhythmic patterning of speech—does not merely make speech
more melodious and euphonious. It lends to speech, as I tried to
show earlier, an extra-linguistic dimension. By the super-imposi-
tion of an aesthetic structure upon the "natural" structure of
language, verse enhances the eloquence of language, enabling it
not only to express more powerfully what prose can express, but
to express what prose cannot express at all.

We all know how character is made manifest in drama—
character, that is, in the sense of moral disposition. Character
in this sense is expressed through the speech, thought, and action
of the agent. Pre-eminently, however, through speech, for speech
not only shadows forth the inner man; it precisely qualifies action.
It seems clear, furthermore, that the finer the instrument of
expression, the better it can convey character in this sense. So

that, while prose will do well enough—will indicate the thought and feeling, the motives and habitual inclinations of the speaker—verse, in the hands of a master, will do better.

The argument is stronger still with respect to the personal aspect of character. For the person, the most existential element in character, is hardly expressible by ordinary speech. Its expression requires an instrument of quite extraordinary power; and this is what Shakespeare possessed in the blank verse of his maturity. I submit, then, that it is just Shakespeare's pre-eminence as a poet that accounts for his ability to create characters who are persons. The poetry, of course, works in conjunction with the unrealistic convention of character presentation which I discussed a moment ago; it gives this convention, in fact, its very life. Periodically throughout his drama, we are given glimpses of the soul in its moments of deepest suffering or charismatic perception—as, for example in Macbeth's

> If it were done when 'tis done, then 'twere well
> It were done quickly. If the assassination
> Could trammel up the consequence, and catch
> With his surcease, success. . . .   (I.vii.1–4)

Only such verse, in its precise control of tone, feeling, and ambiguous implication, could convey the hallucinatory terror of the soul poised precariously between crucial action and revulsion from action. And once the imagination of the specator is so informed, it will not boggle at trifles, but will supply deficiencies from its own store.

V

If Shakespeare's characters are distinctive in the way I have been laboring to define, then this ought to have consequences in terms of the total effect of Shakespearean tragedy. That is, if we respond to persons differently than to individuals, we ought to respond differently also to the stories they enact. We might expect, then, that some of Aristotle's observations about Greek tragedy will not apply, or will apply only in a qualified sense, to Shakespearean tragedy. Take, for example, the dictum that the tragic hero ought to be good, i.e., morally good. We may infer

Aristotle's reason for this, if we remember that he singles out as truly tragic the kind of plot in which a good, but not too good, man passes, because of some error, from happiness to misery.

I take his reasoning to be roughly as follows. To feel pity and fear for the protagonist, the spectator must sympathize with, or identify with, the protagonist. But this is possible only if the protagonist is morally good or, at any rate, not depraved. He must be like the spectator himself, only somewhat better. He must not be too good, for then again he will be unlike the spectator and so unsympathetic. His human frailty, moreover, signified by his error, not only makes him seem more human; it also provides the "cause" of his misfortune, making it appear to be the result of a probable chain of events.

This makes good common sense. Yet if we try to apply it to Macbeth or Cleopatra, it will not do at all. For these characters are not morally good; they are, in fact, quite bad. Must we say then that the plays in which we find these characters are not tragedies? Not at all: This would be to deny the evidence of our immediate response. As a matter of fact, we *do* sympathize with Macbeth and Cleopatra. To account for our sympathy we have to go beyond the common sense of Aristotle and look for an aspect of human character unknown to him. This aspect, as I have been arguing all along, is the person.

Macbeth and Cleopatra are, of course, morally distinct individuals; but they are also unique persons. Our response to them and to their stories, therefore, is a response that transcends, even while it includes, our response to individuals. Insofar as we regard Macbeth and Cleopatra as persons, their moral defects may modify our feelings toward them, but can never quite alienate us. Our sense of their personality overrides, as it were, our repulsion, and so makes possible a kind of tragic plot and tragic effect which Aristotle's pagan wisdom could not have conceived.

The case of *Macbeth* is the more clear-cut of the two plays. The last half of the play has always seemed to me very puzzling. Macbeth degenerates to the point where only a kind of insensate courage remains of the sensitive and noble creature he once was. According to Aristotle, the play should cease to be tragic, especially after the wanton murder of Macduff's family. Then we no longer have a good but imperfect protagonist; we have instead a depraved and evil one. We ought to feel then, not pity and fear, but moral indignation while he lives and relief once he is destroyed. So powerfully realized, however, is Macbeth as a person that we can never for a moment forget what he has been, and what, despite his moral degeneration, he still is. It is in fact just the awful chasm between the person he always is and the beast he becomes that elicits, in his instance, the emotions distinctive of tragedy. Yet this is a kind of tragedy different from any the world knew before Shakespeare.

In a similar way we can understand the paradox of Cleopatra. The critics have never been able to decide quite what to do with Cleopatra. They cannot but deplore her wantonness, her depravity, if you will. On the other hand, they have their fascination to contend with. Is she Antony's *femme fatale,* a lascivious gipsy? Or is she Antony's co-protagonist? I think the latter view is the correct one. Difficulty arises in interpreting the play because of the tension between Cleopatra's moral nature (or, rather, her immoral nature) and the superbly realized person that she is. It is the latter impression which ought to take precedence in our view of her simply because, in the peculiar imaginative world of the play, it is personal relationships that are important rather than moral problems. The play, to put it simply, is about human love and human persons, and the supreme good in such a context is the personal realization that the lovers achieve in bestowing their all on each other. When the action takes place on such a level, moral categories simply do not come into question.

VI

What, finally, is the distinctive effect of the sort of tragedy I have been describing? I do not think it possible to define precisely the extremely complex emotions elicited by Shakespearean tragedy. Pity and fear, to be sure; but something more, something at once more emphatic and elusive. Bradley hints at it, I think, when he speaks of Shakespearean tragic feeling as a profound sense of waste, "the waste of good." We are in a position to name the source of this feeling, even if we cannot describe it directly.

Hamlet, Othello, Macbeth, King Lear, Antony, Cleopatra:

Insofar as these fictive creatures are felt to be persons—unique,
infinitely precious, irreplaceable and irrecoverable beings—just so
far do we feel their destruction to be not only pitiful and terrible,
but a waste of the most precious substance in our experience.
This, I believe, is the distinctive note of Shakespearan tragedy.
Lear strikes it for us when he enters with Cordelia dead in his
arms:

> Why should a dog, a horse, a rat, have life,
> And thou no breath at all? Thou'lt come no more,
> Never, never, never, never, never.   (V.iii.306–308)

Cleopatra strikes it, too, when Antony dies, in a slightly different
key:

> The odds is gone,
> And there is nothing left remarkable
> Beneath the visiting moon.   (IV.xv.66–68)

The finest epitome of this feeling occurs just after Cleopatra
herself dies. Charmian crystallizes in a few lines the elusive and
brilliant light of the play. The startling use of the passive voice
in this passage forges at one stroke the overriding sensation that
it is not Cleopatra who has lost her life, but that it is we who
have lost her—that Phoebus himself is bereft forever of the
privilege of being gazed upon by those magnificent eyes, with-
drawn forever to the brilliant world behind their downy windows.

> Now boast thee, death, in thy possession lies
> A lass unparallel'd. Downy windows, close;
> And golden Phoebus never be beheld
> Of eyes again so royal!   (V.ii.318–21)

NOTES FOR CHAPTER SEVEN

1. The pertinent passages in the *Poetics* are these: "Character is
what makes us ascribe certain moral qualities to the agents . . ."
(6.1450a); "Character in a play is that which reveals the moral
purpose of the agents, i.e. the sort of thing they seek or avoid . . ."
(6.1450b); "There will be an element of character in the play, if . . .

what a personage says or does reveals a certain moral purpose; and a good element of character, if the purpose so revealed is good" (15.1454a).

2. Jacques Maritain, "The Conquest of Freedom," in *The Social and Political Philosophy of Jacques Maritain,* ed. J. W. Evans and L. R. Ward (New York, 1955), p. 14.

3. *Confessions* X.vi–xvii.

4. P. Philippe de la Sainte Trinité, *Études Carmelitaines* (April, 1936). Quoted in M. C. D'Arcy, *The Mind and Heart of Love* (New York, 1947), p. 321.

5. The "impurity" of Shakespeare's dramaturgy, its combining of naturalistic and stylized modes, has clear implications for the Shakespearan actor and producer. The question as to whether Elizabethan acting was naturalistic (as Marvin Rosenberg argues) or declamatory (as B. L. Joseph holds) does not appear to be answerable on the basis of the external evidence so far produced. This evidence seems, indeed, to point both ways. The internal evidence of the plays themselves, however—the evidence of Shakespeare's plays, at any rate—suggests that the acting was mixed, that naturalistic and formal modes alternated with each other in accordance with the mixed styles in the plays. As for production, since the Shakespeare play focuses on language, character, and *inner* action, the most appropriate mode ought to be the most austerely unlocalized and unset.

6. E. E. Stoll, "Source and Motive in *Macbeth* and *Othello*," *RES* XIX (January 1943), 25–32. See also Stoll's *Art and Artifice in Shakespeare* (Cambridge, 1933).

CHAPTER EIGHT

LITERATURE AND BELIEF

I HAVE ASSUMED all along that there is some sort of norm of human nature, the very possibility of communication being grounded, as I see it, on the existence of such a norm. To the extent that men share a common nature, they can put aside their individual quirks and share in understanding works of literature. Yet men differ radically in their basic beliefs, and, since works of literature inevitably imply or embody basic beliefs, we may wonder how such embodied beliefs can fail to interfere with the appreciation of a reader who does not share them. Donne's "Holy Sonnet I" embodies the beliefs of a devout Christian; Auden's "Lay Your Sleeping Head, My Love," those of an atheist human- ist. A good reader, whatever his personal beliefs, can understand and be deeply moved by either poem. How is this possible? The problem would seem definable only if it were formulated in terms of an exemplary and concrete case.

Such a case is ready to hand in the often-mooted question of Christian tragedy. Critics as different as A. C. Bradley and I. A. Richards have maintained that Christianity and tragedy are in- compatible with each other, and no one appears to have chal- lenged this view.[1] R. S. Crane has glanced at the question and ruled it out of bounds. It involves, he says, "a pseudo-issue . . . which really has no identifiable reference outside the game of dialectical counters in which it has arisen."[2] My own view is that the problem itself is real enough and cannot be so easily dis- missed.

Crane himself has made the problem accessible to solution by distinguishing two basic modes of critical procedure. The "ab-

stract", mode begins typically with some hypothesis about literature or nature or men, and then discusses particular works in
terms of this hypothesis. The "matter-of-fact" mode, on the other
hand, begins with the actual literary work and attempts to reason
back to the necessary causes of such a work and the reasons for
its excellence or imperfection.[3] Of the latter method Aristotle is,
of course, the founder and chief exemplar.

Attempts to deal with our problem have usually proceeded by
way of the "abstract" method, and Crane is right, I think, in
suggesting that, so conceived, the problem admits only of an
irrelevant solution or no solution at all. That is, if one conceives
the problem as involving a relation between two abstract essences
("tragedy" and "Christianity"), then the problem is merely logical, its solution depending merely on the working out of the
logical relations between the two concepts. If, however, we for-
mulate the problem in "factual" terms, the problem and its solution become quite different. Thus: Will a spectator who believes
what Christians have traditionally believed respond to actual
tragedies in the same way as a non-Christian spectator, or not?

Or, appropriating Aristotle's definition, we may define a Christian tragedy as a dramatic imitation of a serious and complete
action, *explicitly ordered* with respect to Christian moral-religious
principle. (We cannot yet include in our definition Aristotle's
final cause—the arousal and purgation of pity and fear—because
that is precisely what remains to be decided.) Our problem then
is: Can a Christian tragedy (as just defined) arouse and purge
pity and fear?

To these questions E. I. Watkin has answered an unqualified
"no." Tragedy, he says, involves the tragic conflict,

> and the tragic conflict in turn involves the presuppositions of a
> non-religious interpretation of life. For the tragic conflict is a
> conflict between values, and a waste of values, as seen from the
> natural, purely human and subreligious standpoint. . . . It depends
> on acceptance of the values presented in human experience,
> whether positive or negative, as they are valued by the natural
> man, from his purely human and earthly standpoint, and there-
> fore, implies ignorance of their absolute, their real value. Did
> we *see clearly* the real value, the value for eternity of the objects

of human desire or aversion, or human love or human hate, we
could no longer share the joy and sorrow, and therefore could
not enter into the tragic conflict of those who accept them at
their apparent value.[4]

I think that Watkin begs the question at issue here in two ways:
(1) by assuming that a Christian habitually sees and feels things
under the aspect of eternity, and (2) by assuming that the
capacity so to see and feel things precludes the capacity to respond to them at their natural value. Both assumptions involve
a confusion of logical relations with psychological facts.

Does the Christian habitually respond to things in terms of
final ends? We are speaking, as we must in questions of this sort,
of the "mass" of men, those who, as Aristotle puts it, are neither
very good nor very bad. For the saint, perhaps, purely human
values dissolve in the light of the good that transcends them.
But such detachment is hardly possible for the Christian, particularly when he is engaged in a serious drama. Claudio's response to death is, I think, typical and normative. The Duke and
Isabella have told him how to die. He *knows* how. But his fear
remains: "Ay, but to die, and go we know not where;/To lie in
cold obstruction and to rot. . . ." (*Measure for Measure,* III.i.
117–18)

Watkin's second assumption also involves a view of human
psychology at variance with common experience. One *can,* I
think, respond to things at their natural value while seeing
clearly their value for eternity. Wisdom—knowing the causes
and ends of things—clarifies, rather than blurs, one's perception
of the purely natural. The little wisdom that comes to us merely
through the accretion of age does not render us incapable of
understanding the passions of the young. Such wisdom helps us
to understand passion better, indeed, than those possessed by it.
Nor does such wisdom inhibit our sympathy for the sufferer. It
is the old who know best what the young feel and who offer them
the sincerest compassion. The analogy is, I think, a fair one, for
religious wisdom is, after all, a kind of wisdom, and we are speaking of its possession by human beings.

To consider the effect of a particular tragedy on a Christian spectator, we might begin with *Oedipus Rex,* a non-Christian tragedy whose power will hardly be questioned. Our Christian spectator, according to Watkin, will not be moved to pity and fear by *Oedipus* because he cannot see life on the same terms as its protagonist. But the point that Watkin misses is that Oedipus sees life in terms of *universally experienced realities.* Oedipus (and any normal spectator) suffers and perceives the fallibility of even the finest human intelligence before the inscrutable complexity of life. Oedipus comes to know man's awful ignorance— his blindness—of consequences in his best-intended acts. This is the beast that lies in ambush for the brilliant and confident Oedipus—and this is the beast that lurks in all our jungles. It is surely no disparagement of Christianity to say that Christians may share Oedipus's view of the evils that befall him, to assume, in short, that they possess human feelings. Christianity may endow human nature with potentialities it did not before possess; but it cannot *transform* human nature, and no theologian, so far as I know, has ever claimed that it can.

Turning now to Christian tragedy proper, we find Marlowe's *Dr. Faustus* ready to hand. Since the Christian ought to see life on the same terms as Faustus, we might expect Watkin to admit the play's tragic power. No, says Watkin (p. 47), even *Dr. Faustus* cannot be considered tragic, because "if we once *see* that the highest value is . . . the most real Reality, we see that a man can miss it only by his own freely willed fault, and miss it in the precise measure of his free rejection." This seems to mean, in our own terms, that the Christian cannot identify himself with Faustus and will therefore not feel fear for him. But is not Watkin's Christian grievously prone to pride? The Christian's attitude should rather be that "there but for the grace of God go I."

The chief problem that faces us in *Dr. Faustus* is the arousal of pity rather than fear. For if pity is aroused by undeserved misfortune, and if, for the Christian, Faustus eminently deserved damnation, then the arousal of pity really appears to be impossible. The point I would make here is this: Whatever a Christian may *believe* about Faustus's damnation, he will not *feel* that it is wholly deserved. This is so because, to the "natural" mind, infinite punishment always seems in excess of apparently finite acts; or, more simply, because of the abiding mysteriousness of human sin and divine retribution. That Christians *can* pity the damned is attested by our response to the famous Paolo and Francesca episode of the *Inferno*. The tragic power of the episode is, in part, a consequence of our intense awareness of the lovers' infinite loss. Dante, in his own person, so instructs us when, after hearing the lovers' story, he faints with pity: "as though I were dying," he says.

Despite the magnificence of certain scenes, *Dr. Faustus* does not achieve the power of our greatest tragedies. But this is not a result of Faustus's salvation being brought explicity into question. It is rather a consequence of his scanted characterization—which itself may be a result of the play's emasculation. Faustus impresses us at times as an allegorical figure and cannot, as such, elicit our full sympathy. As a "case," *Dr. Faustus* is inconclusive, for, though it suggests the possibility of Christian tragedy, the possibility is not realized.

It is, I think, Shakespeare's *Hamlet* that makes the most convincing case for Christian tragedy. The play meets our definition of the type squarely: Its action turns on Christian moral-religious principle in a way that the action of *Othello* or *Macbeth* does not. In the latter plays we find an assumption of a general Christian outlook, but in their action Christian principle is not *explicitly formative*. I can make this distinction clearer by summarizing the central action of *Hamlet*.[5]

An acutely intelligent and scrupulous Christian, Hamlet is enjoined by his father's ghost to do what is almost beyond the capacity of flesh and blood: to avenge his father's murder and taint not his own soul. Revenge not only goes against the grain of Hamlet's sensibility; it is especially abhorrent to him because he knows it may involve his own damnation. For revenge is mortally sinful. Even when public justice is unavailable, revenge is justified only if the avenger is explicitly commissioned to act as God's minister and only if he performs his commission without a vestige of personal passion. In view of his feelings toward Claudius, Hamlet's task is well-nigh impossible. His spiritual struggles (his "hesitations," if you prefer) thus stem from the almost insuperable difficulty of avenging his father's murder and saving his own soul.

The initial movement of the play comprises Hamlet's attempt to discover whether the ghost is a "spirit of health or goblin damned." If the ghost is an infernal apparition, Hamlet will be risking damnation by acting on its word:

> The spirit I have seen
> May be a devil; and the devil hath power
> T' assume a pleasing shape; yea, and perhaps
> Out of my weakness and my melancholy,
> Abuses me to damn me. I'll have grounds
> More relative than this. The play's the thing
> Wherein I'll catch the conscience of the King.
>   (II.ii.623–33)

The mousetrap is clearly intended to make sure of the ghost, before Hamlet acts on the ghost's word. "O good Horatio," Hamlet says after the King betrays his guilt, "I'll take the ghost's word for a thousand pound." And this is the issue that obsesses Hamlet until that revelation. It is the subject, I think, of Hamlet's best-known soliloquy (III.i.56 ff), which a long critical tradition has maintained to be about suicide.

But even after Hamlet is sure of the ghost, he still faces the possibility of damnation if he acts in a spirit of personal vengeance. And he comes perilously close to this. When, after the mousetrap, Hamlet finds Claudius at his prayers, he does not kill him—for the wrong reason. He will wait, he says, until he can be sure of sending Claudius's soul straight to Hell (an intention that appalled Dr. Johnson). But if he *did* kill Claudius with such an intention, he would almost certainly damn himself. There is thus a double irony in his *not* killing Claudius at this time, for, as we learn at the end of the scene, Claudius's prayers were inefficacious, and, if Hamlet had killed him then, he *would* have sent Claudius' soul (and his own), to Hell.

The killing of Polonius in the next scene is, as Fredson Bowers shows, the turning point of the play. In killing Polonius rashly and wrongly, Hamlet becomes both minister *and* scourge, i.e., a sinful instrument of God's justice—as he himself realizes. The murder, he knows, will set him packing; and he knows too that he "will answer well the death I gave him." He knows he is a doomed man.

The mood of Hamlet and the tone of the play now move in the direction of Christian resignation. Dimly at first but with increasing clarity, Hamlet perceives that the way to his goal lies, not in action—in taking all responsibility upon himself—but in putting himself into the keeping of God's Providence. "Let it work," he remarks of the plot laid for his life; he will delve below these mines. But when he returns to Elsinore he is a changed man. His indiscretion *has* served him well: He has learned of the "divinity that shapes our ends," and has realized that "the readiness is all." This is the mood which is brilliantly expressed in the graveyard scene. The scene points up not only the vanity of mortal glory but the futility of Hamlet's earlier attempts at action. Everything and everyone finally come to dust. Possessed of such a vision, Hamlet achieves the detachment which makes his task possible. He carries out his commission and, perhaps, saves his immortal soul too.

My summary leaves out of account a good deal in the play. It leaves out the pervasive honor theme. Hamlet being a Renaissance Prince as well as a Christian, his sense of honor comes into direct conflict with his Christian ethical sensibility. It also leaves out Hamlet's skepticism and energetic rationality—which make for further complication. Yet the central action of the play seems to me accurately, if barely, indicated by my summary. And if the play *is* thus structured, it meets squarely our definition of Christian tragedy. There can be little question of the play's tragic power—especially for a Christian spectator. For not only death threatens Hamlet; damnation threatens him too. The tragic emotions are thus aroused with respect to both natural and supernatural evils. The final movement of the play, moreover, facilitates that acquiescence which Bradley discerned as proper to the close of a tragedy. Hamlet's own resignation in Act V promotes detachment in the spectator (especially in a Christian spectator) and thus enables him to see the play as a meaningful whole, to see the underlying order which "justifies" the terrible events he has witnessed and imaginatively engaged in.

My thesis is supported, finally, by certain theories about the origin of tragic drama. I refer to the tracing of Greek drama back to ancient religious rituals, in which was enacted the destruction and rebirth of the Year Spirit. The tragic hero, as we know him in the Greek plays that have come down to us, embodies strangely contradictory qualities. Oedipus, for example, is both innocent and terribly guilty. By suffering for unwilled and unintended crimes, he cleanses—"purges"—society, and so makes possible its material and moral rebirth. Such a hero's make-up, says Gilbert Murray, is

> quite in accord with the strange but well-known confusion which exists in the Bacchic ritual and the sacramental feast. Is it the god himself who is torn and devoured, or is it the god's enemy? To avoid the horror of murdering your god, you can say that the figure you tear is the enemy Pentheus and not the god Dionysus; but you know in your heart that it is only the life of Dionysus himself that will have any true magical effect, and you show your knowledge of this by arranging that the image which you call Pentheus shall be shaped and dressed in every detail so as to be like Dionysus. . . .
> Put briefly, it seems that historically the tragic hero is derived both from the Life Spirit . . . who comes to save the community with the fruits of the New Year, and from the polluted Old Year . . . who is cast out to die or to wander in the wilderness, bearing with him the sins of the community.[6]

Now if these primitive meanings inform the tragic hero (I believe they do), then the Christian martyr ought to be an excellent tragic hero. For the martyr is, from one point of view, a scapegoat figure: By his innocent and supererogatory suffering, he "purges" the Mystical Body. The viability of the martyr as tragic hero and the potency of martyrdom as tragic plot are, I think, "proved" beyond question in Carl Dreyer's film *The Passion of Joan of Arc* (1927). The complex emotion which this film elicits is strikingly similar to that which Murray describes as proper to Greek tragedy. Murray contends (p. 65) that, we feel love for the tragic hero because he is a saviour, "a brave man fighting and suffering to redeem those who without him would be lost; we feel horror toward him because of his sins and pollution, and their awful expiation. And both feelings must have been intensified in ancient tragedy by the subconscious memory that the sins he expiates are really ours."

This is precisely the sort of double consciousness and ambivalent response that Dreyer appeals to and elicits. His camera cuts continually from "supernatural" to "natural" scenes and back again—playing these perspectives against each other so that we see the action simultaneously as one of acute human suffering and of spiritual progress toward apotheosis. Especially at the climax, when Joan is at the stake, the camera turns from Joan and focuses with extraordinary power and "rightness" on those anonymous faces in the crowd with whom we have become identified; and those faces, in momentary, extreme close-up, run the gamut of strictly human response: terror, awe, hysteria, grief. Since the film demands both a religious and a purely human response, it is, I think, tragic for both Christian and non-Christian. But it is also more profoundly tragic for the Christian. Which leads me to conclude not only that Christian tragedy is possible but that its possibilities are greater than those known or envisaged by Aristotle.

One hesitates to generalize too far in matters such as this; yet certain extensions of our conclusions seem to me legitimate. We may fairly say that what is in question in matters of belief in literature is not some abstract logical problem; what is involved is a set of human feelings and attitudes attendant upon some intellectual position. What needs to be determined in any case is how far a particular belief circumscribes or inhibits a human being's capacity to see and to feel.[7] This means that we can never say *a priori* which beliefs are viable in literature and which are not. We have to judge the execution, as Henry James was fond of saying. We have to estimate for each work how the beliefs embodied in it either facilitate human feeling or interfere with it. And we have to estimate how far the reader may be "persuaded" by the poet's art to believe for the moment what, outside the fictive world of the work, he may not believe.

What ultimately *enables* belief in literature is, of course, its fictionality. The rest is up to the poet. It is up to him to make his fictive action such that we may participate in it. Just so far as his art persuades us to believe in his fictive world, so far we may willingly suspend our disbelief and virtually embrace the beliefs embodied in that world.

NOTES FOR CHAPTER EIGHT

1. See, for example, E. I. Watkin, *Poets and Mystics* (New York, 1953), pp. 42–47; and Laurence Michel, "The Possibility of a Christian Tragedy," *Thought* XXXI (Autumn 1956), 403–28.

2. R. S. Crane, *The Languages of Criticism and the Structure of Poetry* (Toronto, 1953), p. 37. Richard B. Sewall in *The Vision of Tragedy* (New Haven, 1959) seems to stand on both sides of the question. At one point (pp. 156–57) he agrees with Michel that "the incompatibility of tragedy and Christianity is inescapable," and goes on to say that he uses the term "Christian tragedy" only as a "useful way of referring to tragedy written in the Christian era which bears the mark of Christian thought and feeling, however short it falls (and to be tragedy, it always does) of the doctrines of the Church." Elsewhere (p. 53) Sewall seems to approach my own position: "Instead of negating tragedy, or taking man in one leap of faith 'beyond tragedy,' Christianity in actual practice, historically, has provided a matrix out of which has come, since the beginnings of the Renaissance, a prodigious amount of tragic expression, not only in literature but in painting, sculpture, and music." This last phrase makes it clear that Sewall does not think of tragedy as a determinate dramatic genre. The issue can therefore never be precisely joined.

3. *The Languages of Criticism*, pp. 23–25.

4. *Poets and Mystics*, pp. 42–43.

5. My interpretation of *Hamlet* is indebted to I. J. Semper's pioneer study, *Hamlet Without Tears* (Dubuque, 1946) and to Fredson Bowers' "Hamlet as Minister and Scourge," *PMLA* LXX (September 1955), 740–49.

6. *The Classical Tradition in Poetry* (Cambridge, Mass., 1927), pp. 64–65.

7. Cf. I. A. Richards, *How to Read a Page* (New York, 1942), p. 170; ". . . there are certainly very different sorts of believings.

Ordinarily we discuss the matter as though the only question were *which* statements should be believed, as though belief were some standardized product, and as though the only question is as to *what is believed*. But *how* and *with what kind of belief* and *as what* are we to believe some statement are more searching questions.... We should beware of supposing that believing or not is like turning a light on or off. It is much more like focusing the eyes." (Richards' italics)

CHAPTER NINE

PROSPECTS

THE MIMETIC THEORY of literature which I have tried to develop in these essays provides, I believe, a more nearly adequate conceptual framework for the study of literature than other theories The theory slights neither the work's intrinsic nature nor its "external" relations. Understood as a form of *mimesis,* the literary work shows us two faces: On the one side, it is *an* imitation, a thing-in-itself with its own proper laws of being and excellence; on the other, it is an imitation *of* human feeling and thus related to something outside itself. The theory thus enables us to steer clear of the dilemmas posed by the neo-classical doctrine of verisimilitude or (at the other extreme) the New Critical doctrine of contextual purity.

Understood as a form of *mimesis,* the literary work has another dual aspect: It is in one sense the experience which its words imitate; in another sense it is the words which imitate that experience. The critic aware of this duality may focus his attention on the words, or on the experience, or on the relation between the words and the experience. Much old-fashioned criticism focused on the experience, and it was faulty at times in not "controlling" itself by its relation to the words of the work. But some modern criticism has equally great faults—I am thinking of the sometimes brilliant criticism of Empson, which tends to regard the words on the page as ultimate. This leads to brilliant irrelevancy—the discernment of verbal or rhetorical ingenuity which has no relation to the experience imitated by the work.

It is apparent that once we introduce "experience" as the ultimate object of imitation, we have also introduced moral judgment as an important element in literary judgment. And the two-faced

117

nature of literature means that evaluation itself may focus either on the words, on the medium, or on the experience. And the validity, the value, of the experience will determine all. If the experience is trivial or falsified, we may speak of that triviality or falsity in terms of ordinary experience, *or* we may speak of the defects of language which embody that triviality and falsity. Strictly speaking, the moral and technical defect is one and the same defect, or, to put it differently, there is a moral dimension to technique.

An additional virtue of mimetic theory lies in its conceiving of genres as historically derived norms of human feeling. In this way it coincides with Croce's idea of poetry as lyrical intuition. Yet the theory permits, as Croce does not, a rational critical procedure, for it sees this intuition articulated ("externalized") in the various literary forms, there objectified and made available to critical understanding and analysis. The genres, understood as intersubjective norms, not only facilitate the production of literary works; they also make it theoretically possible for criticism itself to exist, for the genres provide an object—an intersubjective norm—with reference to which intelligible public discourse can occur.

The process of identification (or partial identification) figures in a number of discussions in this book. I suspect there is no really adequate word for this process. It is not subject to scientific description or examination, being known only through introspection or "intuition." But that such a process (and a human faculty corresponding to it) exists seems to me undeniable. The process is involved, I believe in many fundamental human activities. It is patently necessary, for example, for any human communication that goes beyond the purely scientific or mathematical. It is a way of knowing which does not depend on discursive reason; it is an intuition of the other which is direct and unmediated by logical thought. It is a *sine qua non* of literary experience. And it is probably an important element in what Keats thought of as the artistic personality.

I have spoken a good deal of feeling, of the affective component of literary experience. Some readers may be disturbed by what they may regard as my rampant indulgence in the affective fallacy. I can only plead that, as I see it, the analysis of the affective side of literature involves no fallacy at all if it is properly done. The critic inevitably faces the task of construing both the fictive emotions in the work and the real emotions elicited by it. There is, of course, an uncontrolled impressionism which makes of the work a mere stimulus for the expression of personal attitude and private sentiment. But that is not what I would recommend or practice. The analysis of feeling (I have insisted) must be guided by the assumption of norms of human feeling and controlled by the perception of its object, the form of the work.[1]

The task of dealing with the affective side of literature cannot, in any case, be evaded. One may use "objective" or purely cognitive descriptive terms; but this only submerges the affective element and removes it from control and understanding. Our response to literature, like the object of that response, is neither purely cognitive nor purely affective, but both at once. And criticism must deal with that total response.

Our response to literature is elicited in two fundamental ways, related respectively to the two kinds of *mimesis* (which constitute the basic "duality" of the theory). The reader or auditor participates in the work first of all because of its representativeness, its credibility. His participation is proportional to the work's excellence as an analogue of experience. Through partial identification with the chief character or characters of a play or novel, with the speaker of a lyric, the reader imaginatively participates in meaningful (i.e., formed) human experience. And the quality of his response (other things being equal) is a function of the quality of the work.

But this accounts for only part of the reader's response and involves only one of the processes which elicit it. Part of that response is a function of rhythmic *mimesis*, which is articulated by the temporal patterning of feeling. Partially identified with, say, Hamlet, the reader responds from moment to moment to the events in which Hamlet engages. This temporal pattern is a form of rhythmic *mimesis*. This rhythmic structure clearly takes its shape from the work's representative structure; for the reader's

response at any particular point is determined by what is represented at that point. Yet the rhythmic structure is also different
from the representative structure—even though the reader's response to both aspects of the work (ideally) forms an ultimate
unity of thought and feeling.

When Aristotle speaks of the effect of tragedy, he does not tell
us whether he is referring to the emotions aroused during the play
or after the play is over. It seems clear, however, that a complete
response—what criticism attempts to analyze and understand—
must involve both elements. It must include our perception (facilitated by detachment) of the meaning of the play as a representative *mimesis*. This is a kind of contemplative vision at the end
of the play in which the play is seen "all at once," "spatially." In
addition, a complete response must include the pattern of feeling
which the play has elicited in the course of its performance (our
response to it as a rhythmic *mimesis*). Each component will, of
course, modify the other.

Now most criticism tends to focus on the representative side of
literature, because criticism is by nature detached and "rational."
The process of analysis is more easily conducted when one can
regard its object as a timeless and spatial entity. The representative, furthermore, can be understood more readily than the
rhythmic in familiar moral and rational terms. And so the rhythmic structure of literature tends to be neglected, and we get a
partial criticism, criticism that sees the work "from the outside"
as a purely spatial structure, rather than as the temporal structure it partly is.[2] The rhythmic structure of literature is, to be
sure, very difficult to deal with. Just as verse rhythm is almost
impossible to describe adequately, so the larger rhythm of the
work as a whole presents formidable problems for the critic in-
tent on accurate analysis and description. Not the least of these
problems is the almost complete absence of terms and concepts
with which rhythmic structure might be described.

Yet something might be done. There are, generally speaking,
two modes or "styles" of critical discourse. One is cool, rational,
detached, analytic; it eschews emotional involvement with the
work and aims at precise and "objective" description of repre-

sentative structure and the cognitive implications of that structure. This is the typical style of our time. The other is rather old-fashioned and is not in much favor today. It is frankly emotional, rhetorical, and synthetic rather than analytic. It aims to re-create the experience of the work rather than to analyze it. It is a dangerous sort of criticism, for it is open to many abuses. Yet in its capacity for utilizing all the resources of language to describe the literary work, it holds the possibility also of dealing with rhythmic structure. The best example of this kind of criticism that I know is De Quincey's famous essay "On the Knocking at the Gate in *Macbeth*."[3]

A mimetic theory of literature (let me say finally) accounts for the fundamental seriousness of literature. For if literature is an imitation of human action, then its importance is proportionate to the importance of life itself, or to the importance of the aspect of life with which it deals. Not that literature teaches in the usual sense. But it does keep alive the values of a culture and sustains civilized life quite as much as do laws and other institutions. It does this by habituating its readers to think and feel in a civilized way. According to Aristotle, feeling—the pleasure and pain that ensues on human acts—is a sign of character or moral disposition. In training the feelings of the young in this way we give them actual moral sensibility. We ought, says Aristotle, "to have been brought up in a particular way from our very youth . . . so as to both delight in and be pained by the things that we ought; for this is the right education."[4] Nothing, I think, can better educate in this way than good literature.

There is, of course, a sense in which the study of literature can be too serious. One may come to value literature and the activities that surround it more highly than life, to which it is always subordinate, in the way that all studies are "ornaments" rather than ends in themselves. Even teachers of literature may take themselves too seriously. Their main task does not involve teaching in the usual sense; they are professors of a knowledge which, strictly speaking, cannot be taught. They have, strictly speaking, no subject matter; they have only a corpus of literary works, of whose value they are more or less convinced, and the obligation of making those works known.[5]

To do this we proceed, of necessity, by indirection. We train our students in the interpretation of linguistic and literary signs and symbols; we present to them what is relevant out of our stock of literary and historical knowledge. If we are doing our work well, we will always keep in our mind's eye that experience of the work itself toward which our discursive knowledge only lights the way; and we will be wary of allowing our scholarship or our criticism to usurp the place of the work itself. That is our abiding temptation, our peculiar form of intellectual pride.

NOTES FOR PROSPECTS

1. John Crowe Ransom (*The New Criticism* [Norfolk, Conn., 1941], p. 20) puts the matter well: "Emotion may be keen and piercing, or it may be massive and overwhelming, but these terms are figurative and almost valueless in distinguishing one emotion precisely from another. The specific quality of any emotion is all but indefinable in pure emotive terms, and that seems to be because the distinctness that we think of as attaching to an emotion belongs really to the object towards which we have it."

2. Angus Fletcher remarks that "an adequate definition of mimesis will depend on an idea of poetic rhythm.... Aristotle's stress on action is a stress, inevitably, on rhythm...." ("Utopian History and the Anatomy," in *Northrop Frye in Modern Criticism,* ed. Murray Krieger [New York, 1966], pp. 48–49.)

3. The Shakespeare criticism of G. Wilson Knight should also be cited. It will be readily apparent that my distinction between two critical styles is essentially a rephrasing of Knight's distinction between "criticism" and "interpretation." What puzzles me about Knight is that, though he writes brilliant re-creative criticism, he espouses a spatial theory of Shakespearean dramaturgy. See *The Imperial Theme,* pp. 19–20; and "On the Principles of Shakespeare Interpretation," in *The Wheel of Fire* (London, 1930), esp. pp. 1–6.

4. *Nicomachean Ethics* II.3.1104b (Trans. W. D. Ross).

5. One method of teaching—the audible reading of poems—appears to me especially commendable in the light of these observations. Yet none of our graduate schools, to my knowledge, provides this sort of training. Learning to read Donne or Stevens aloud and skillfully has the virtue of focusing attention on the work itself as an auditory object, while promoting awareness of the relation between its form and meaning and of the more delicate relation between its being and its value.

INDEX